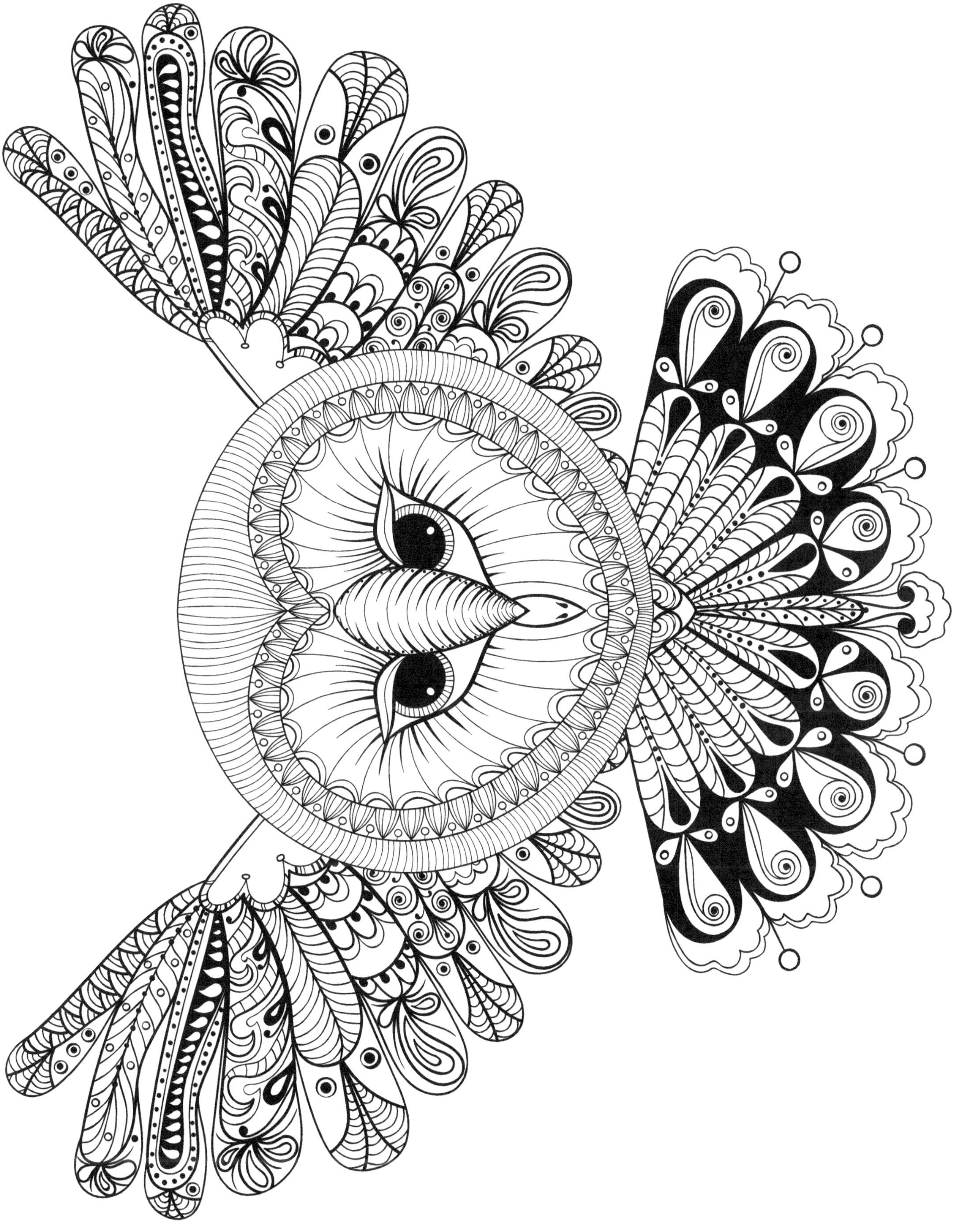

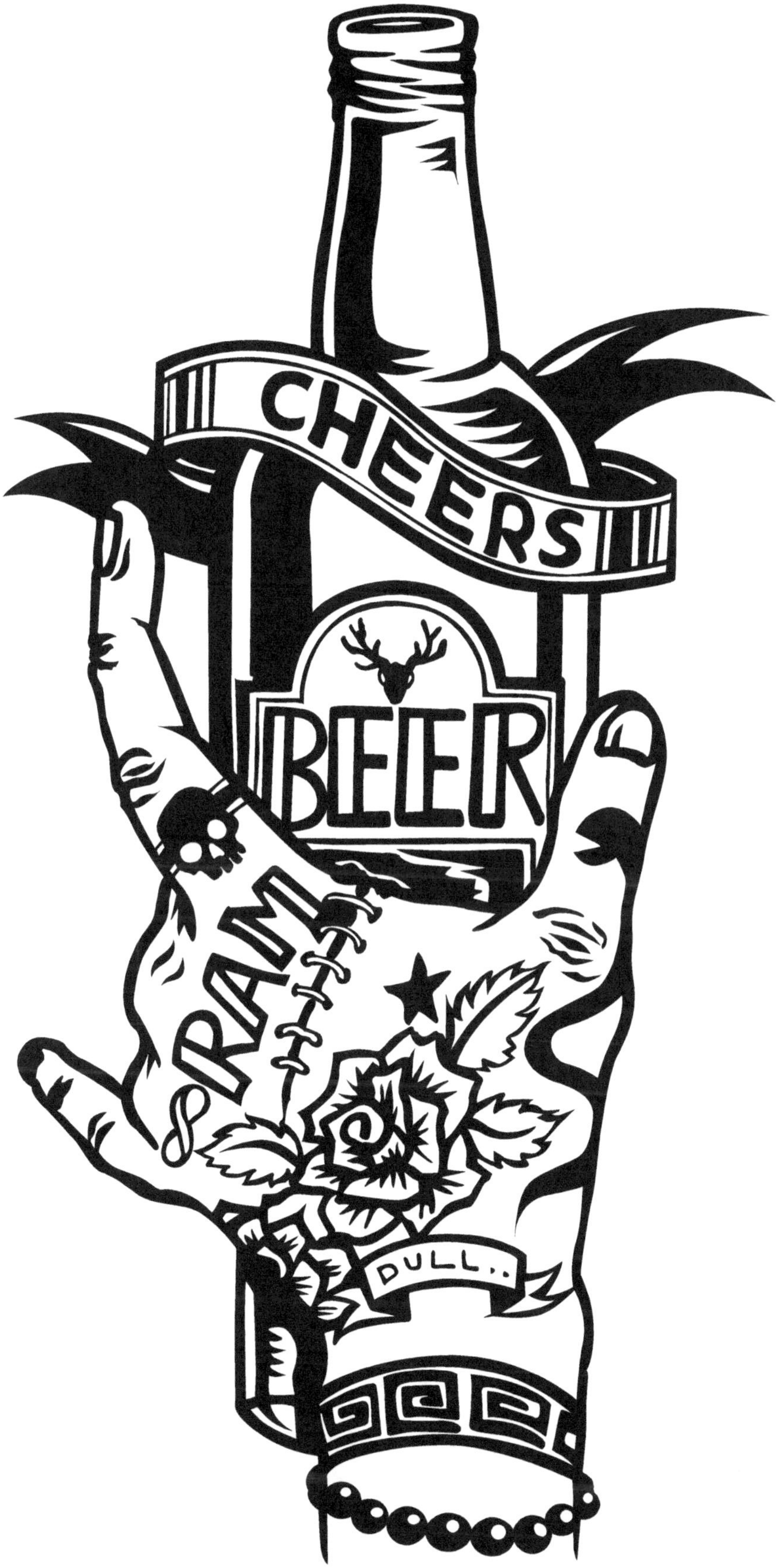
CHEERS
BEER
RAM
DULL..

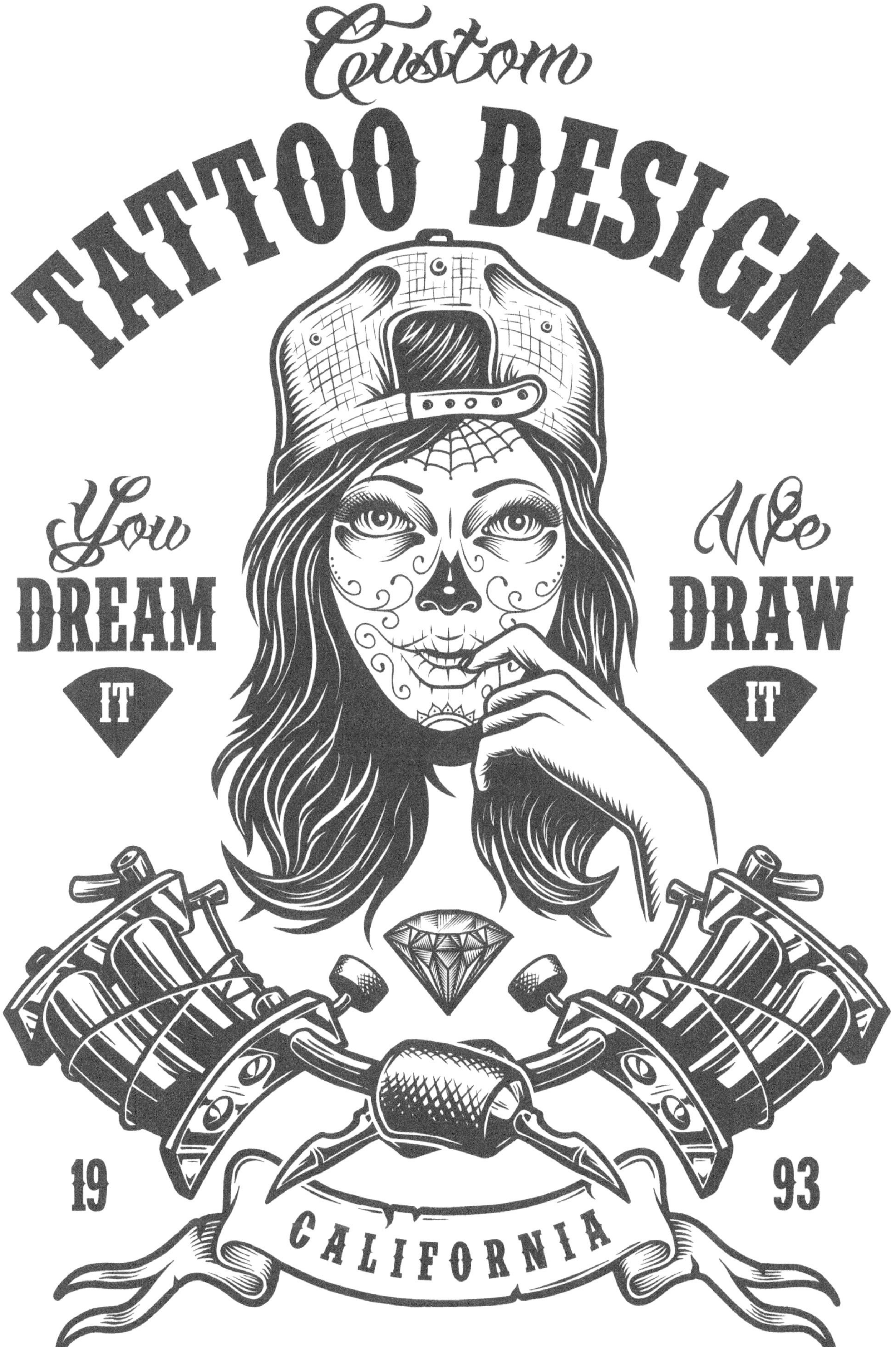
Custom
TATTOO DESIGN
You
DREAM
IT
We
DRAW
IT
19
93
CALIFORNIA

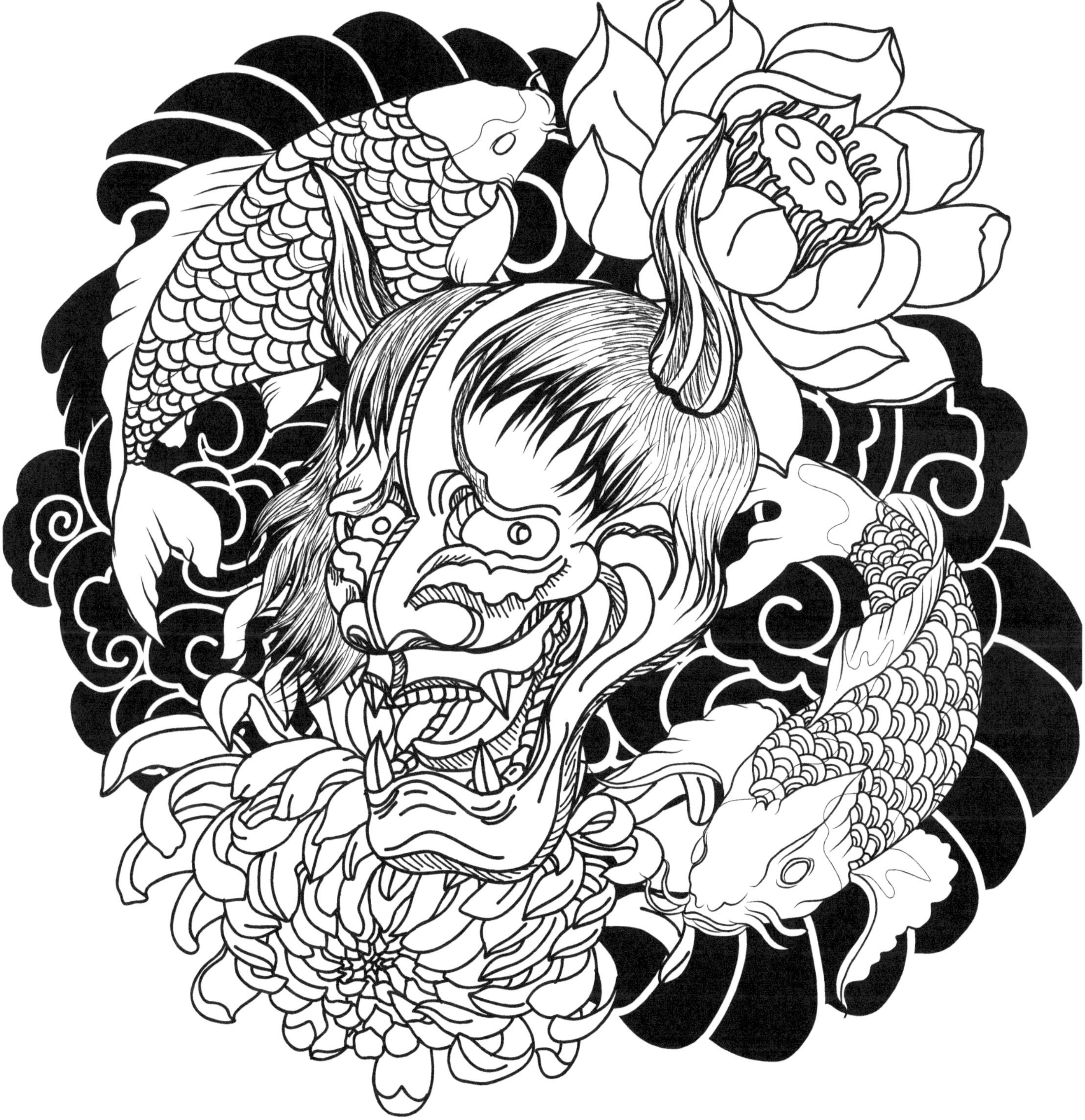

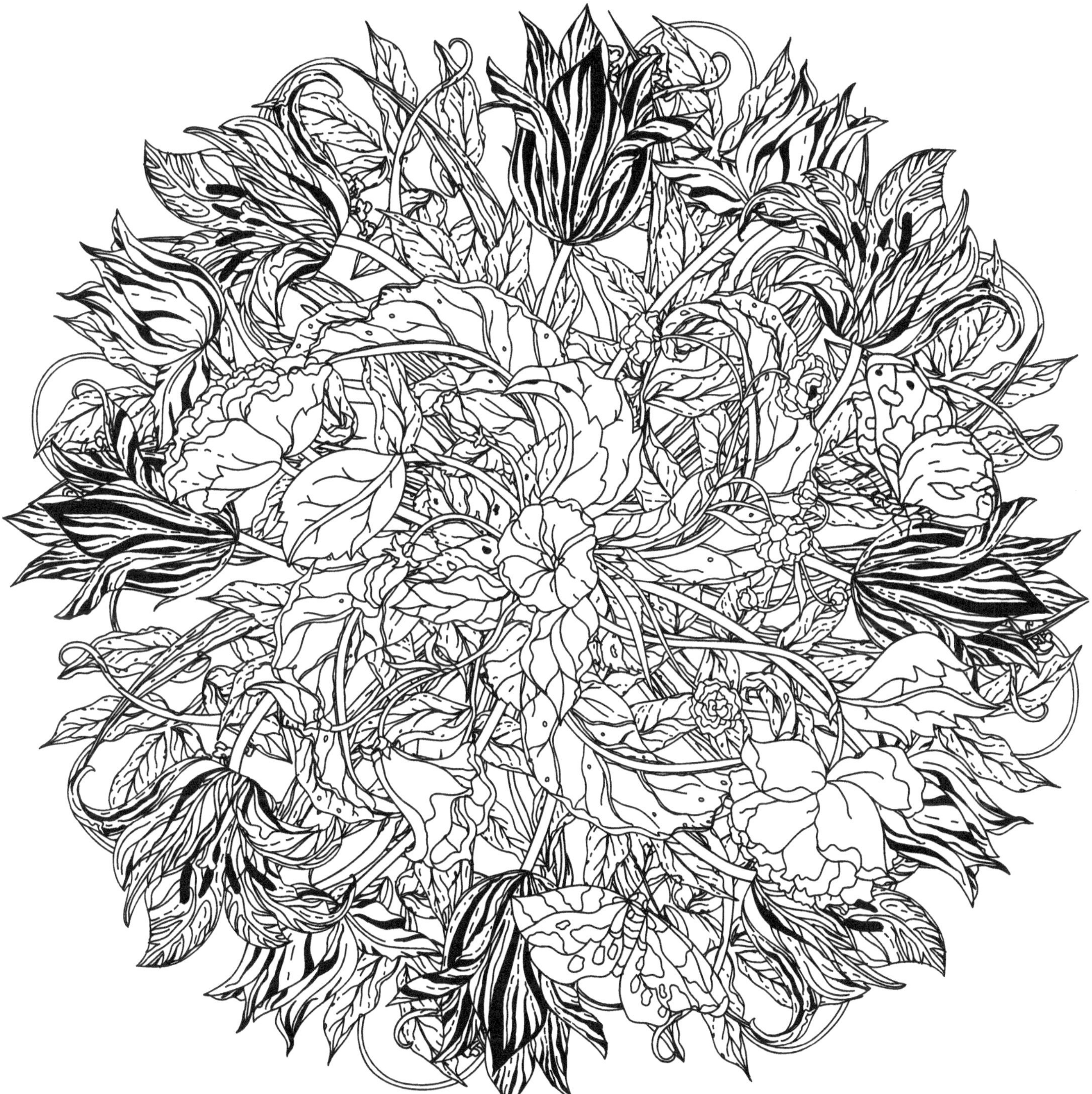

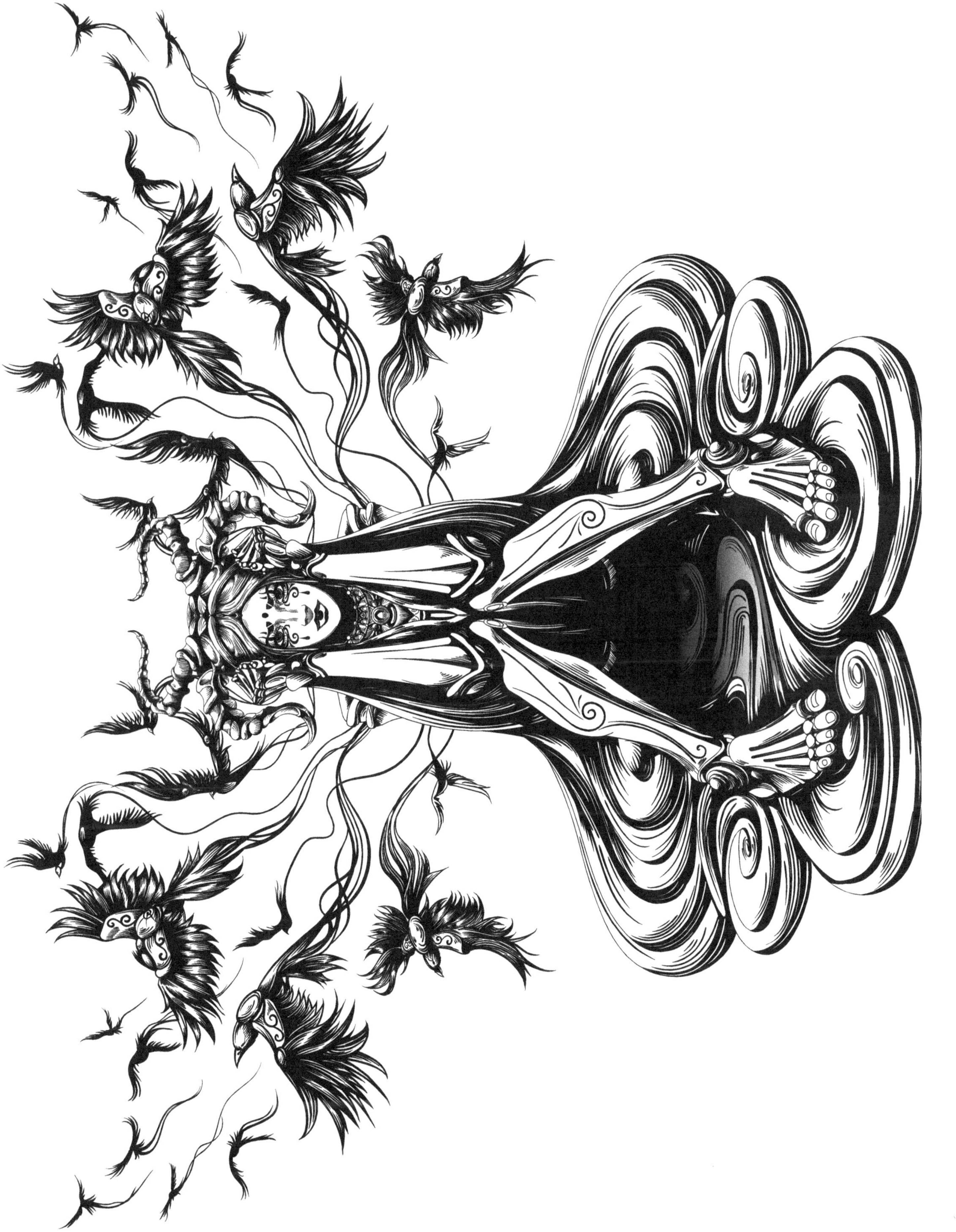

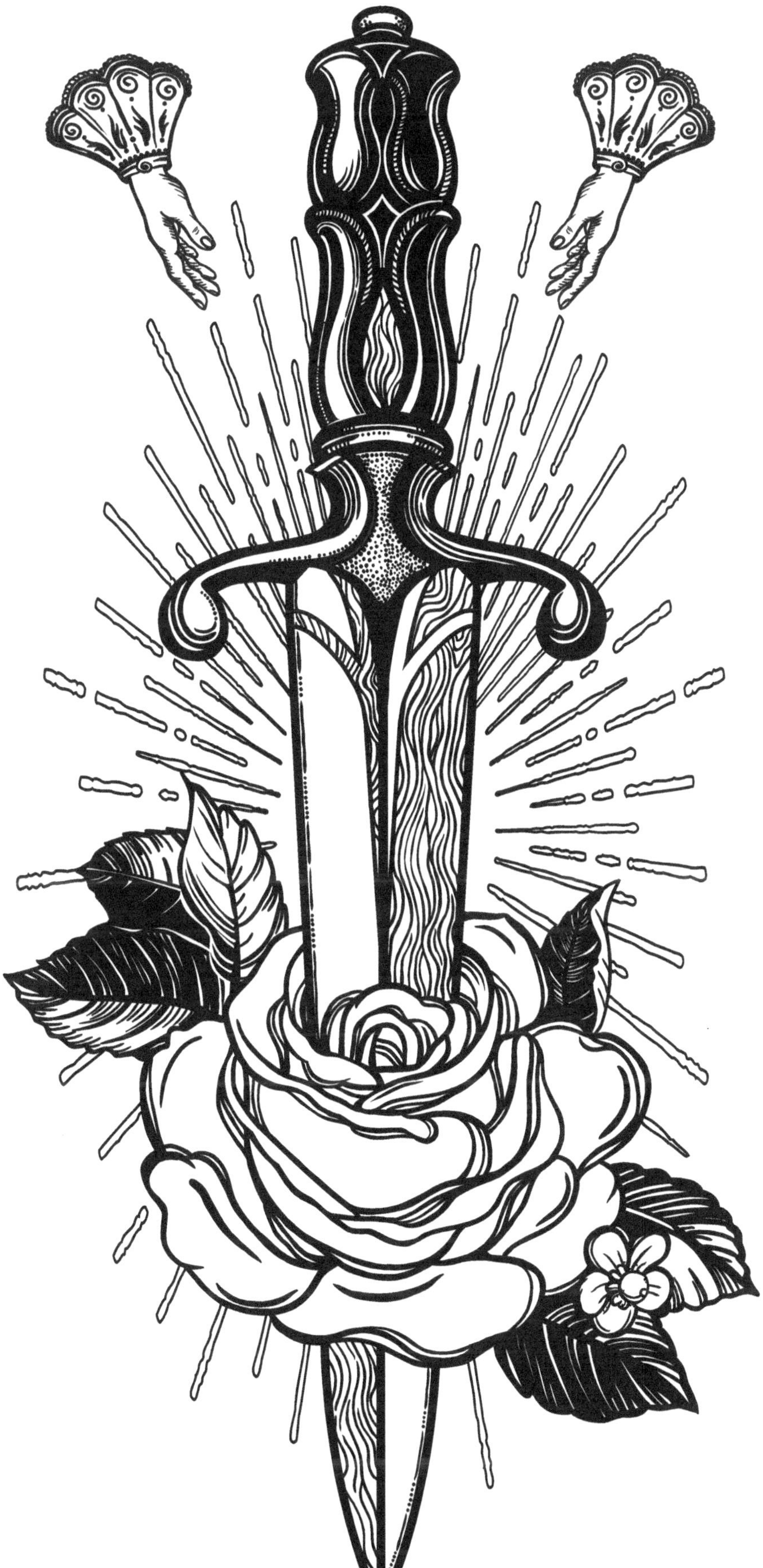

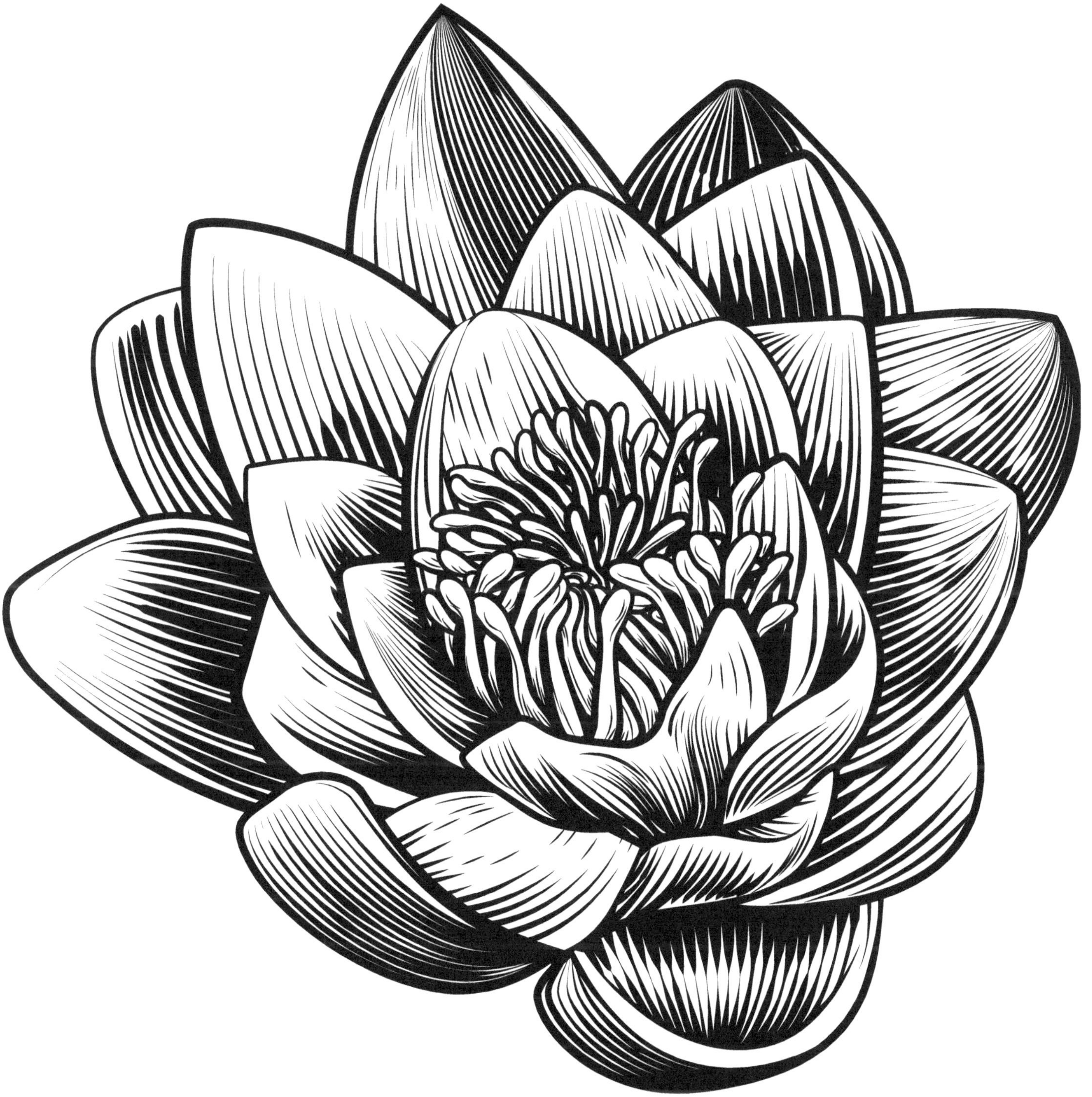

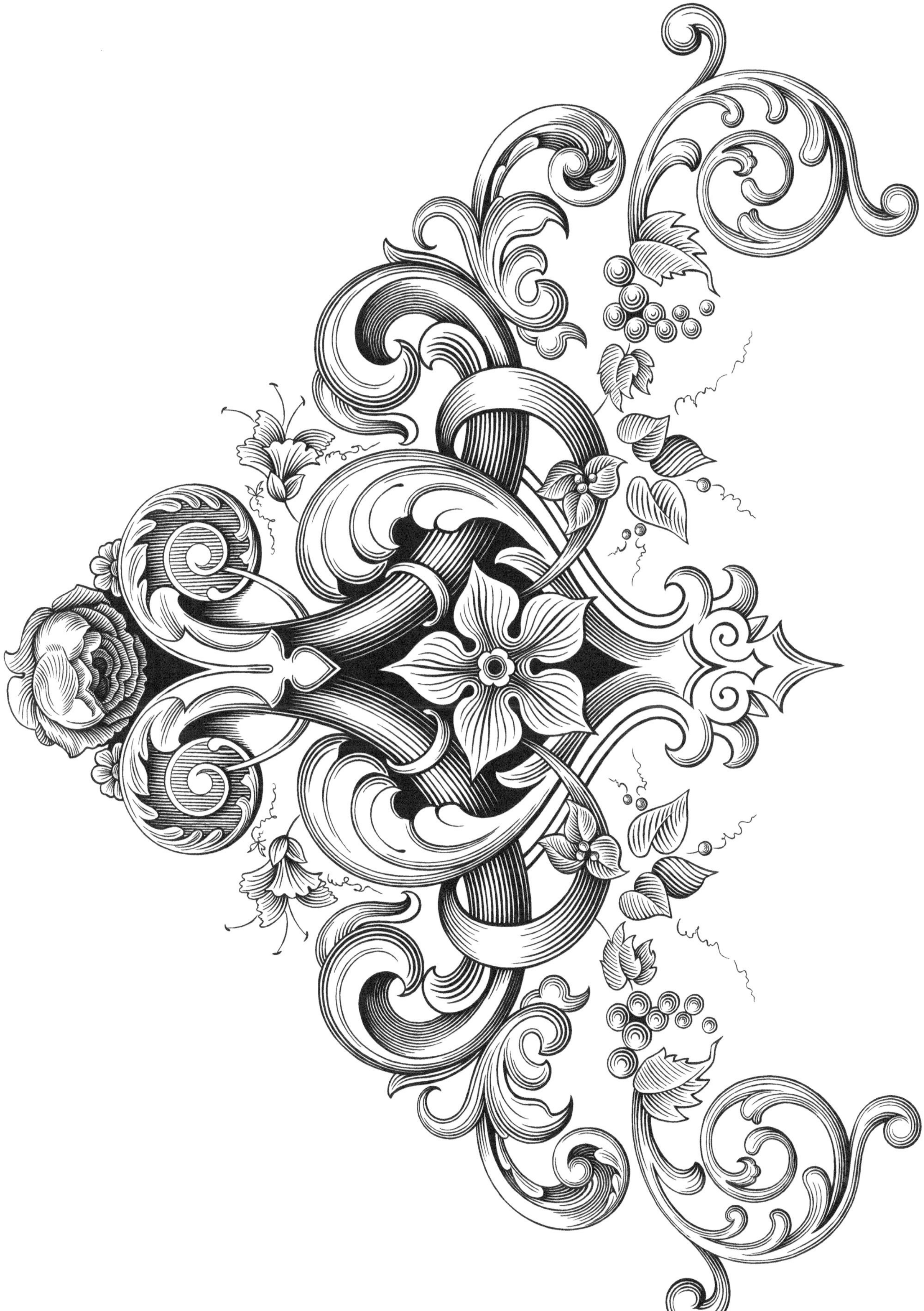

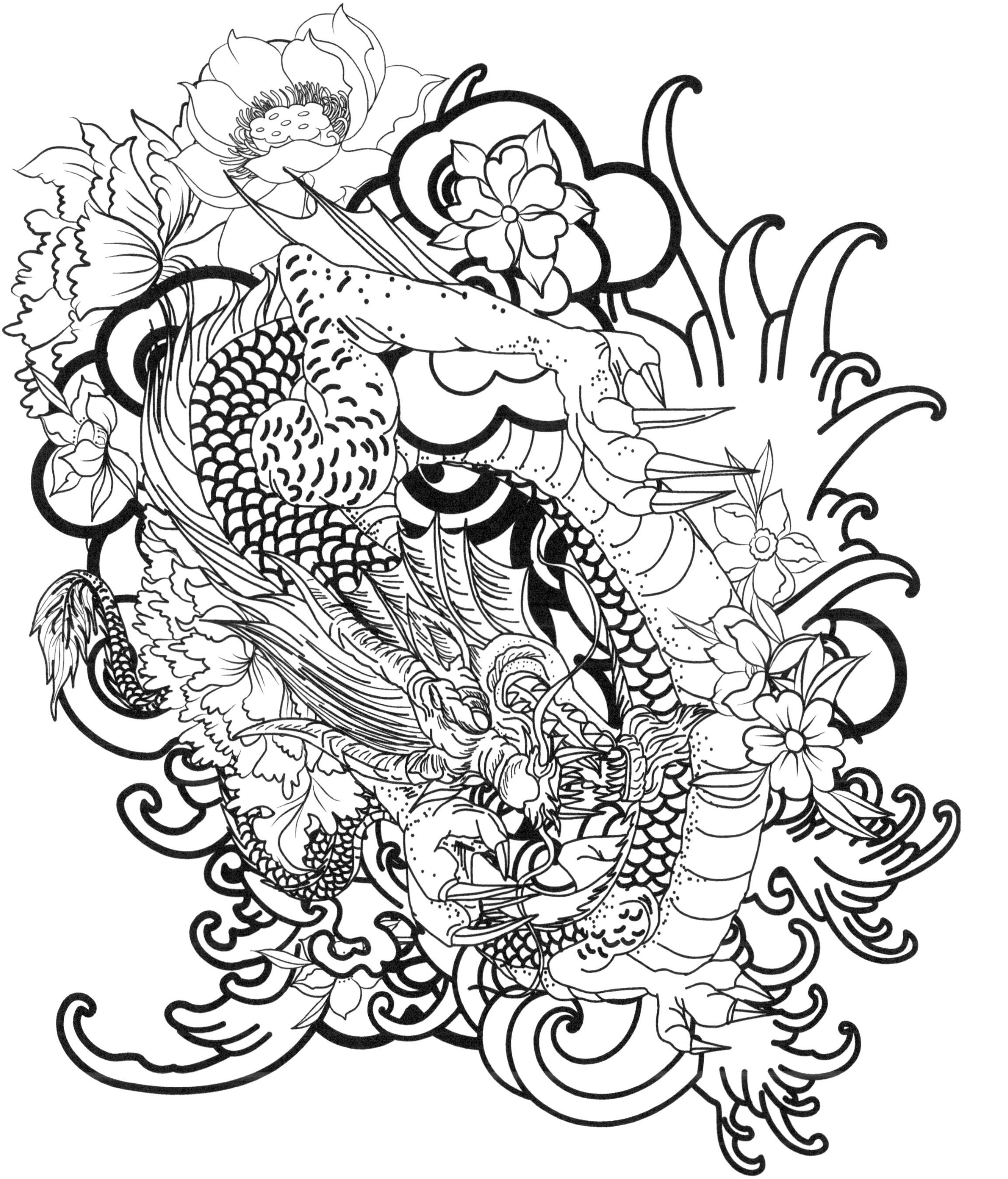

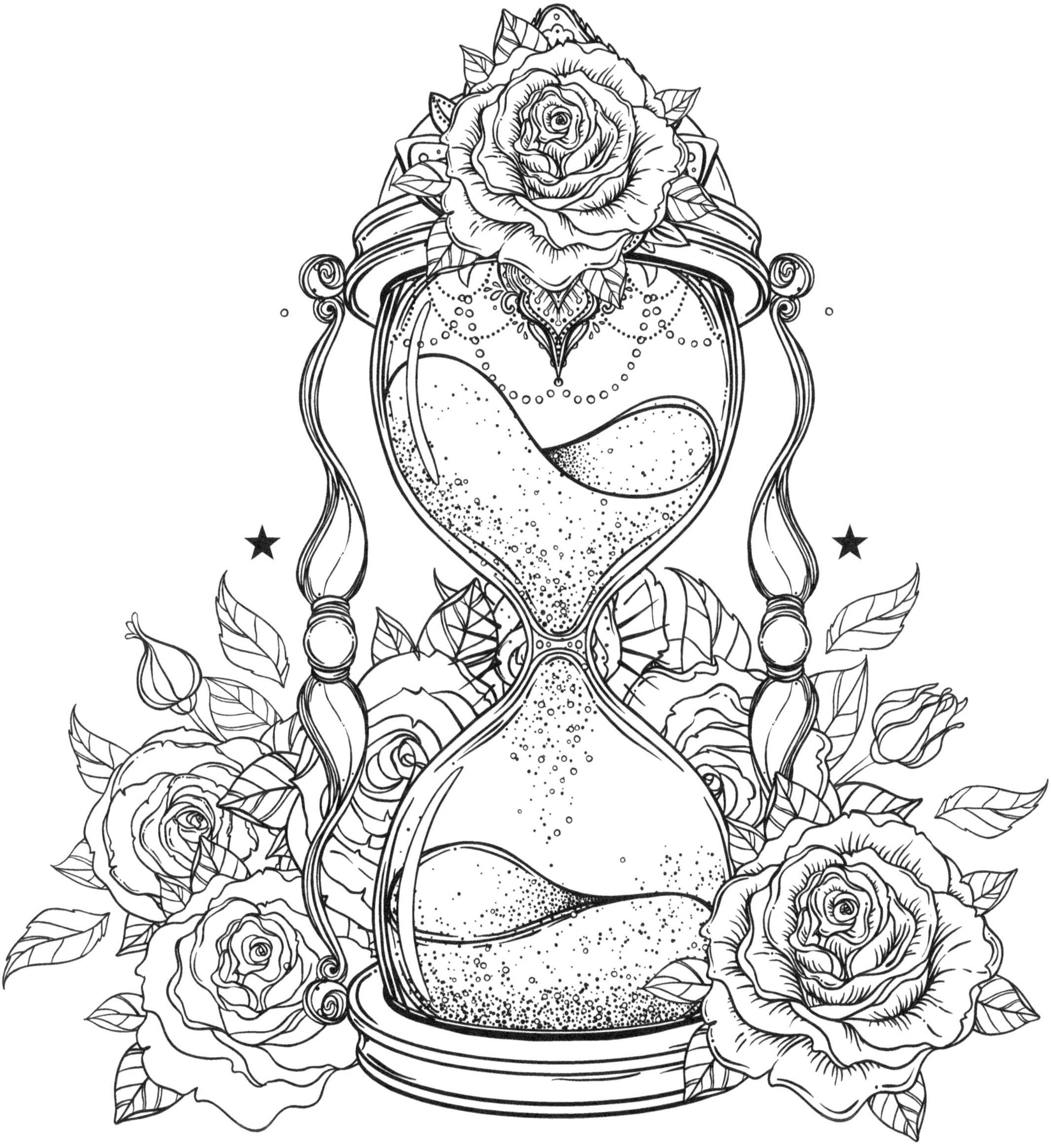

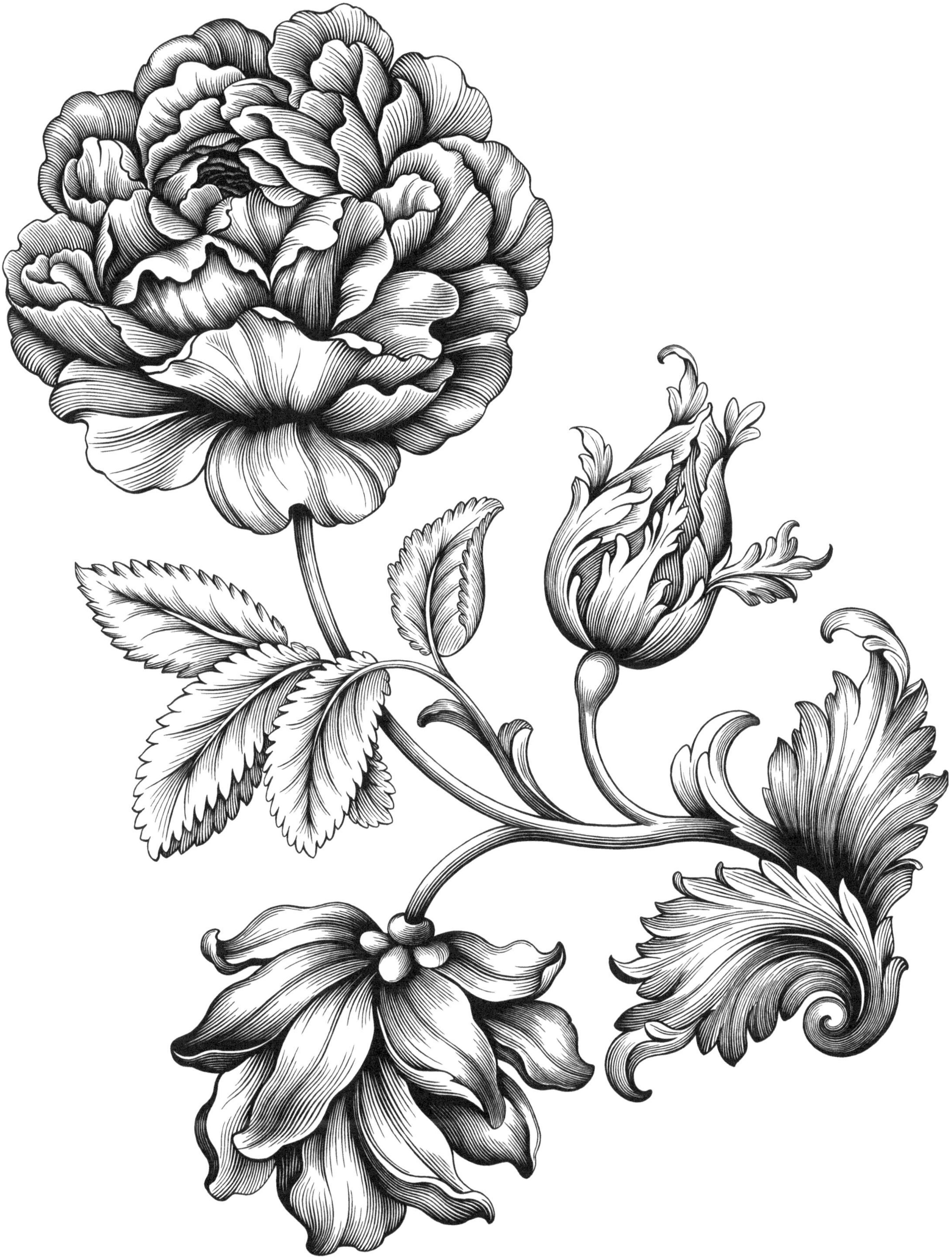

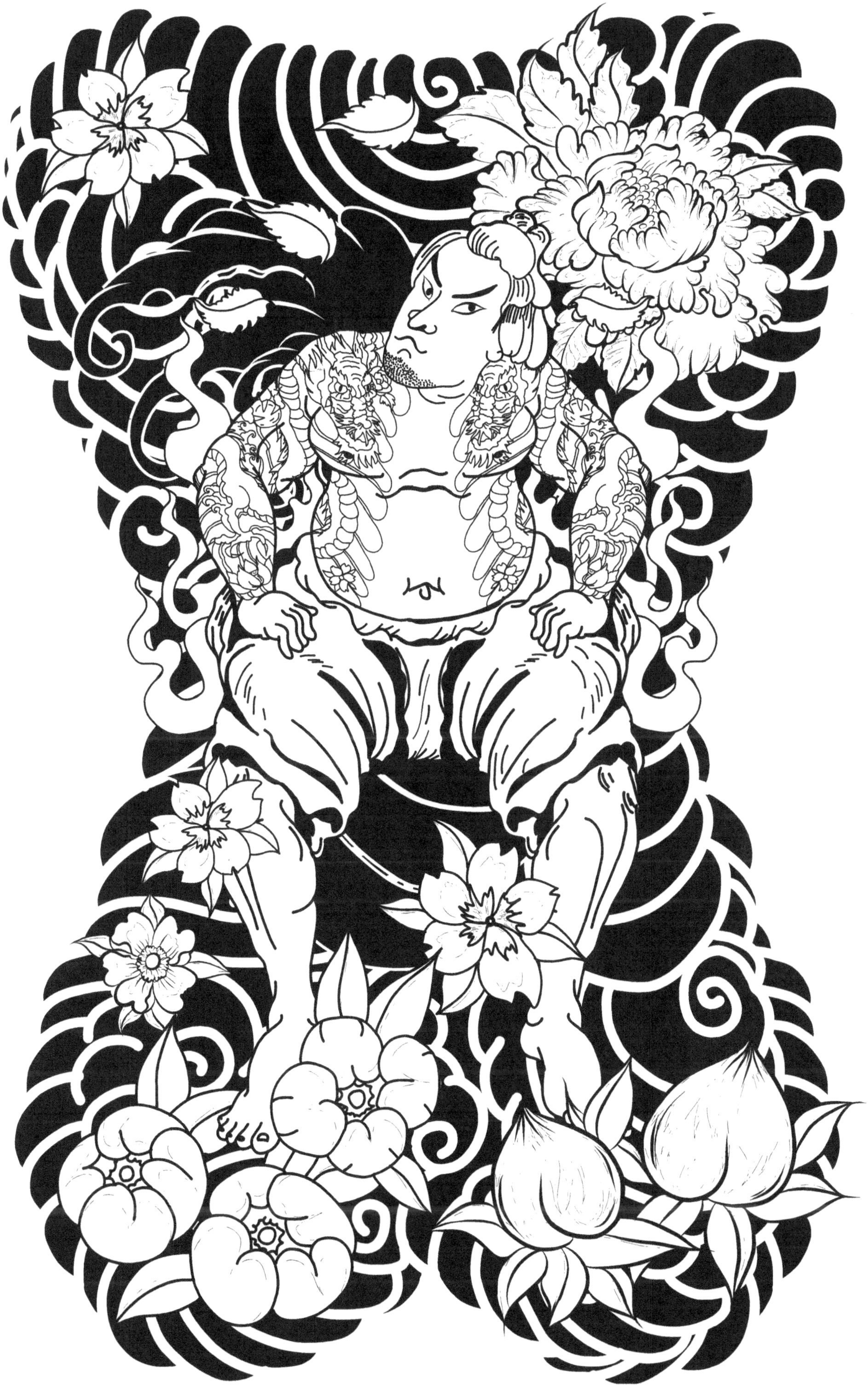

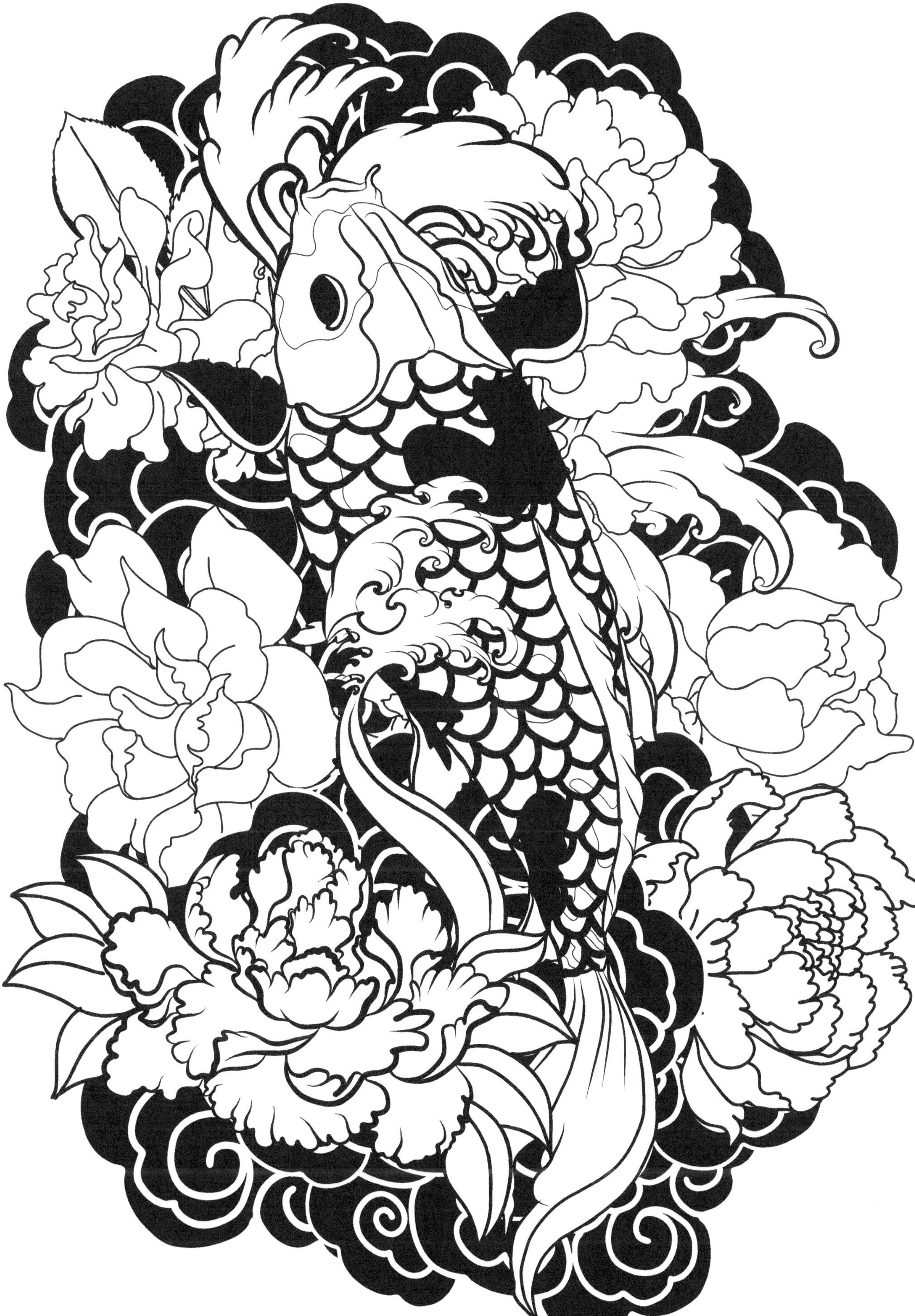

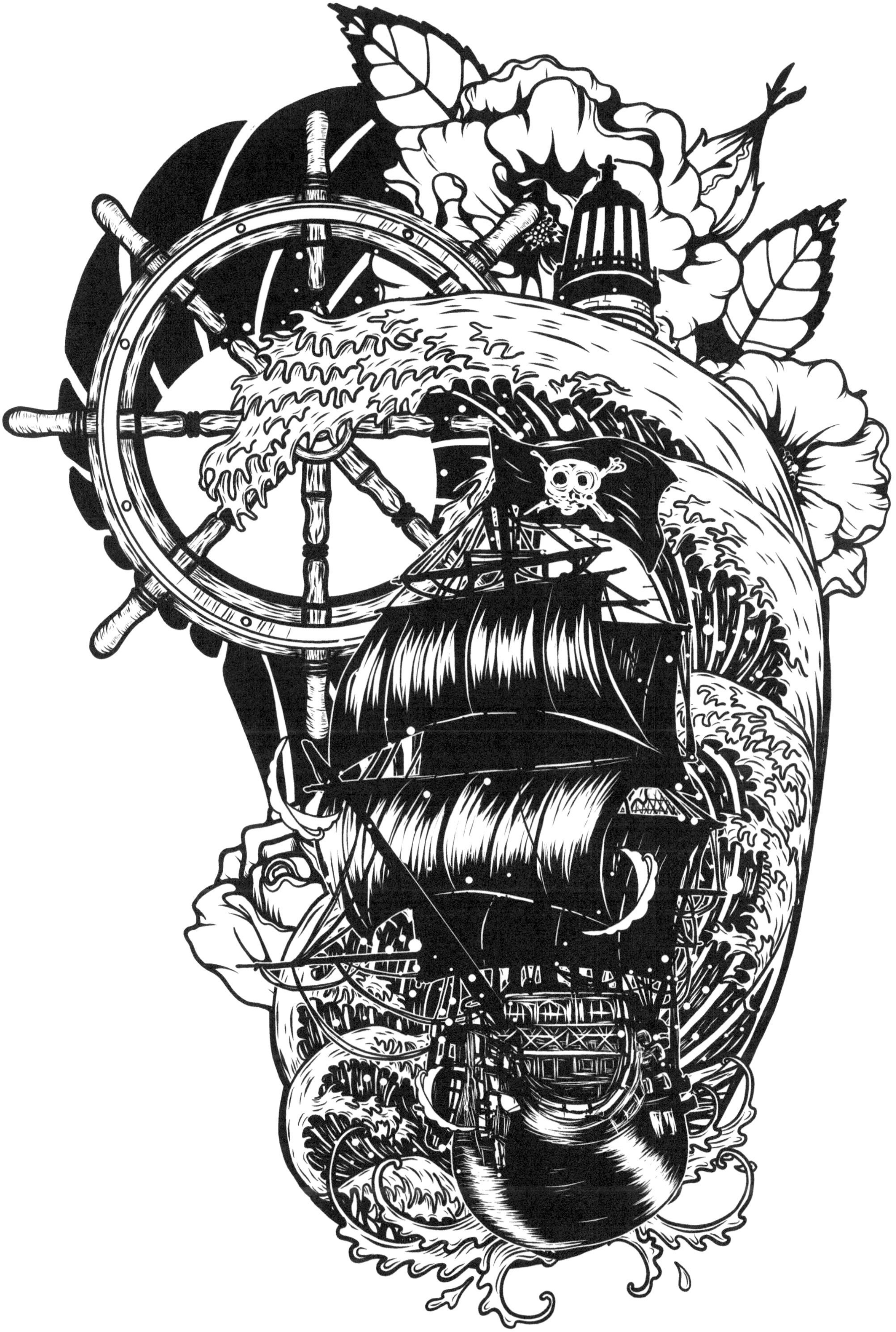

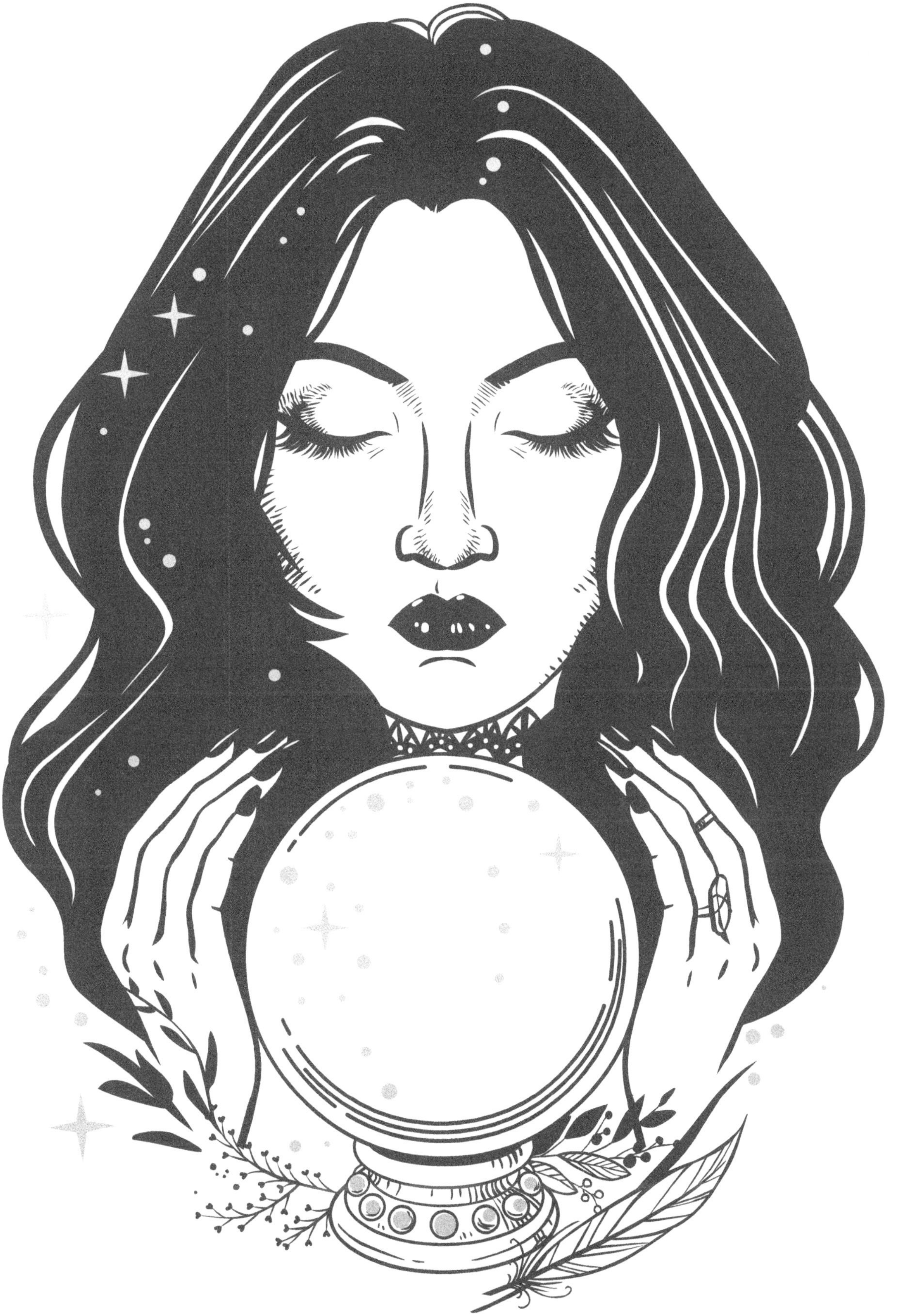

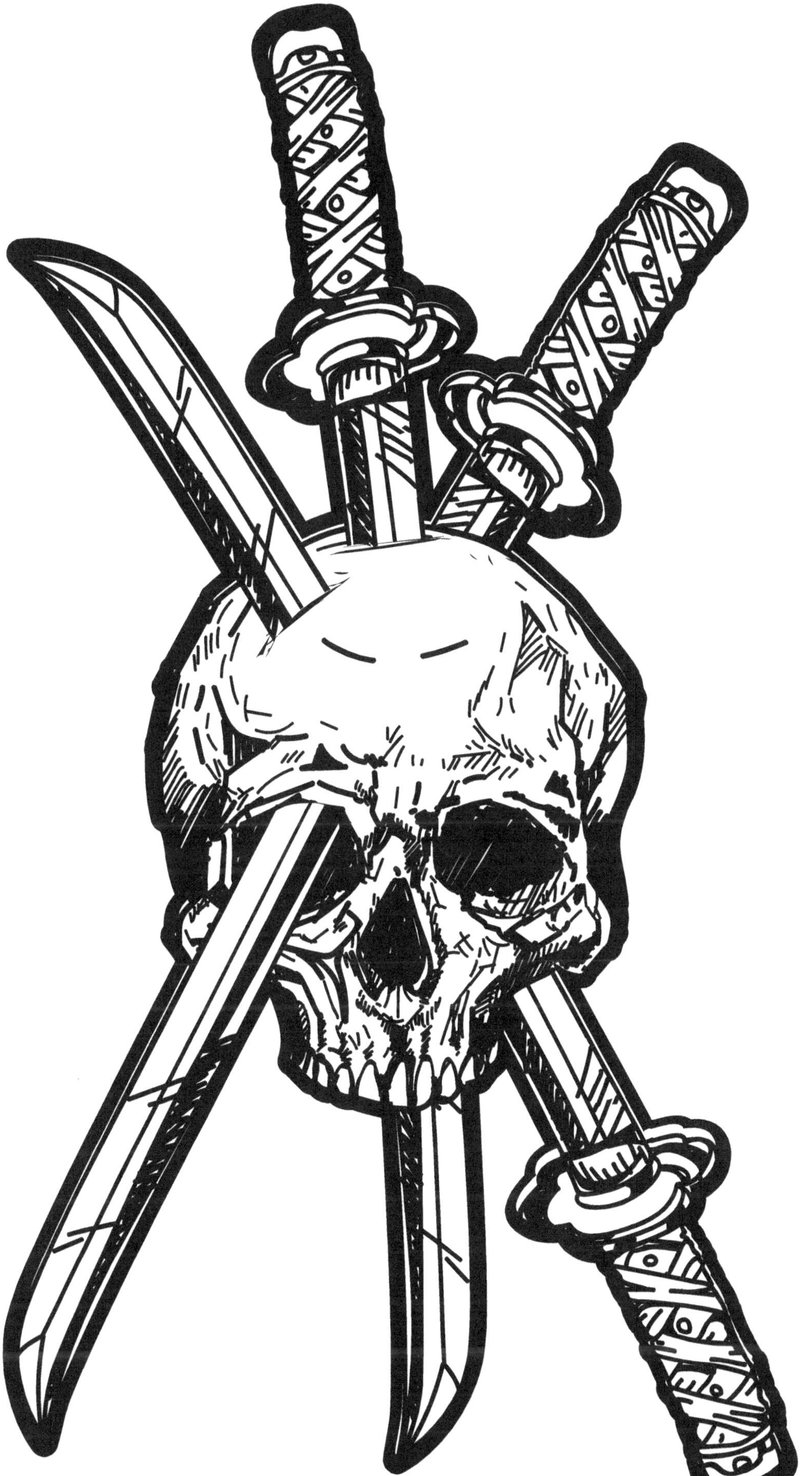

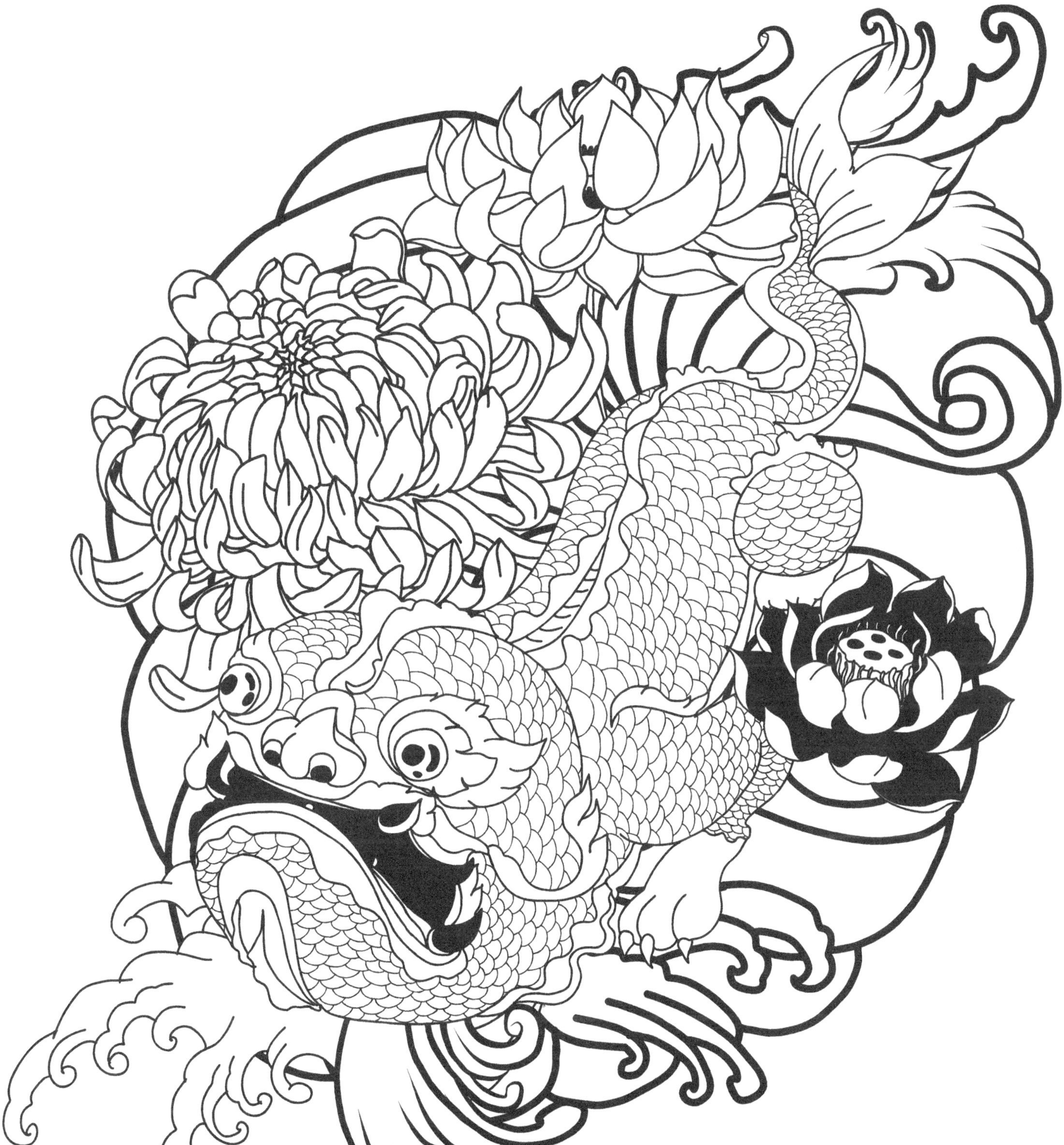

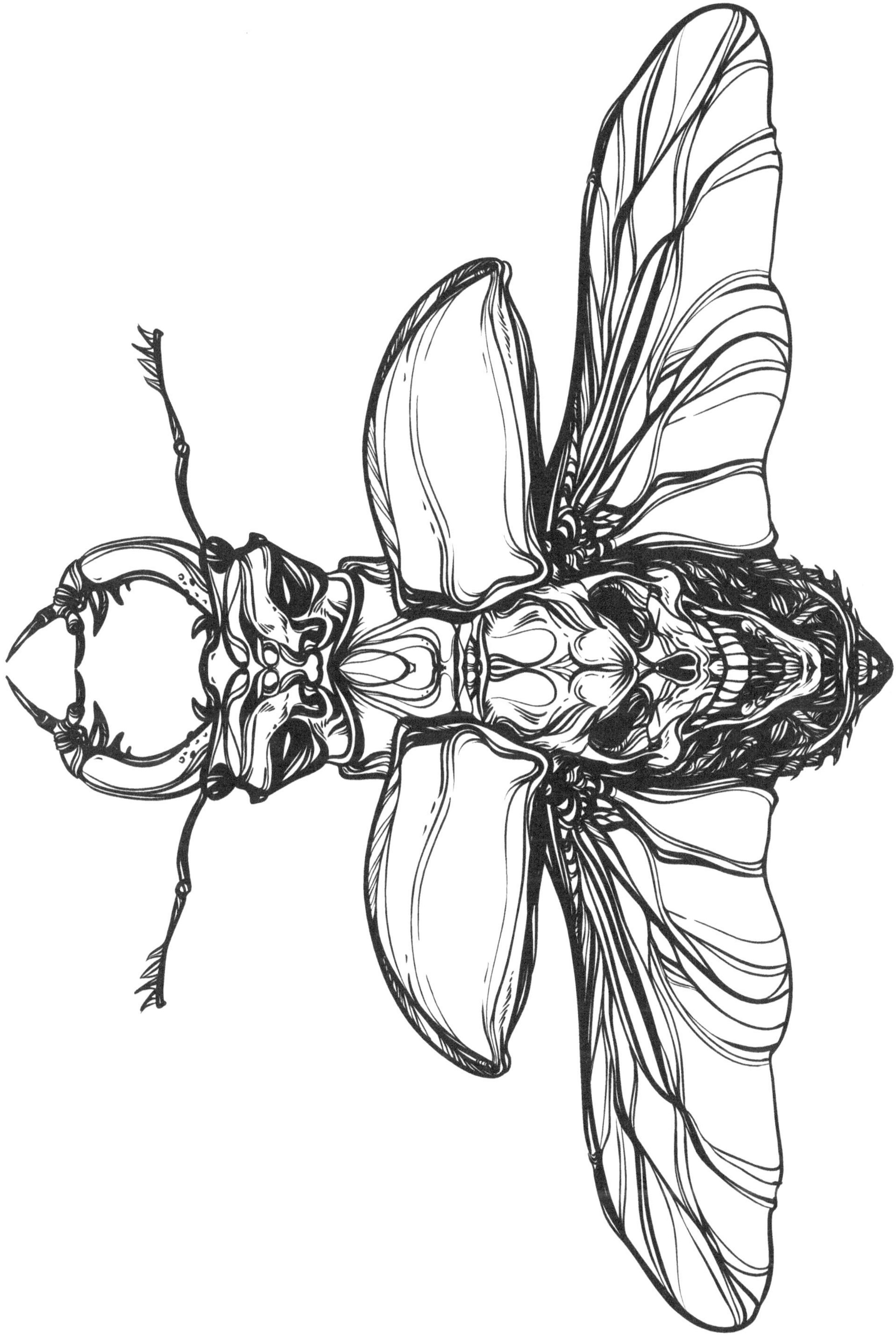

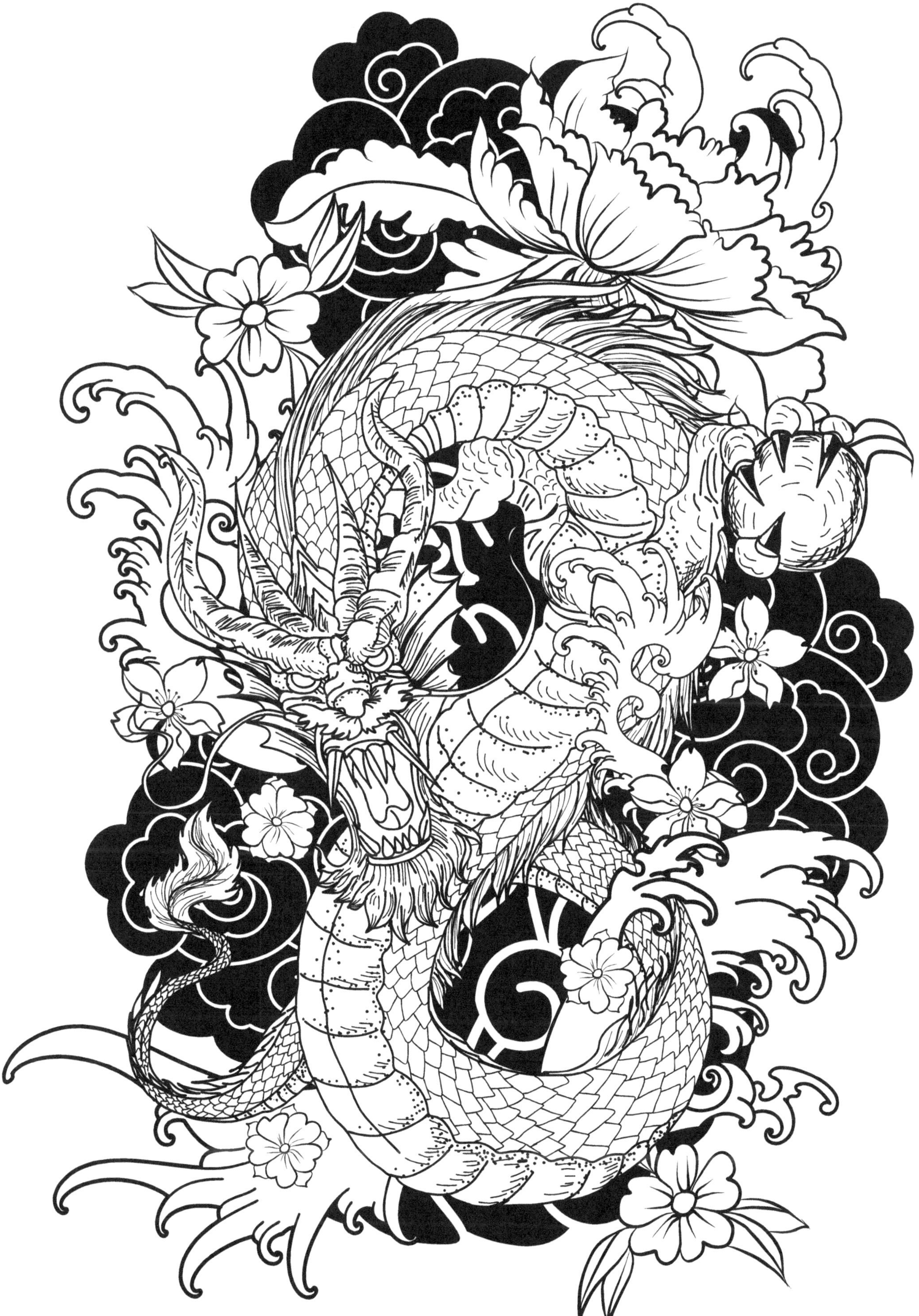

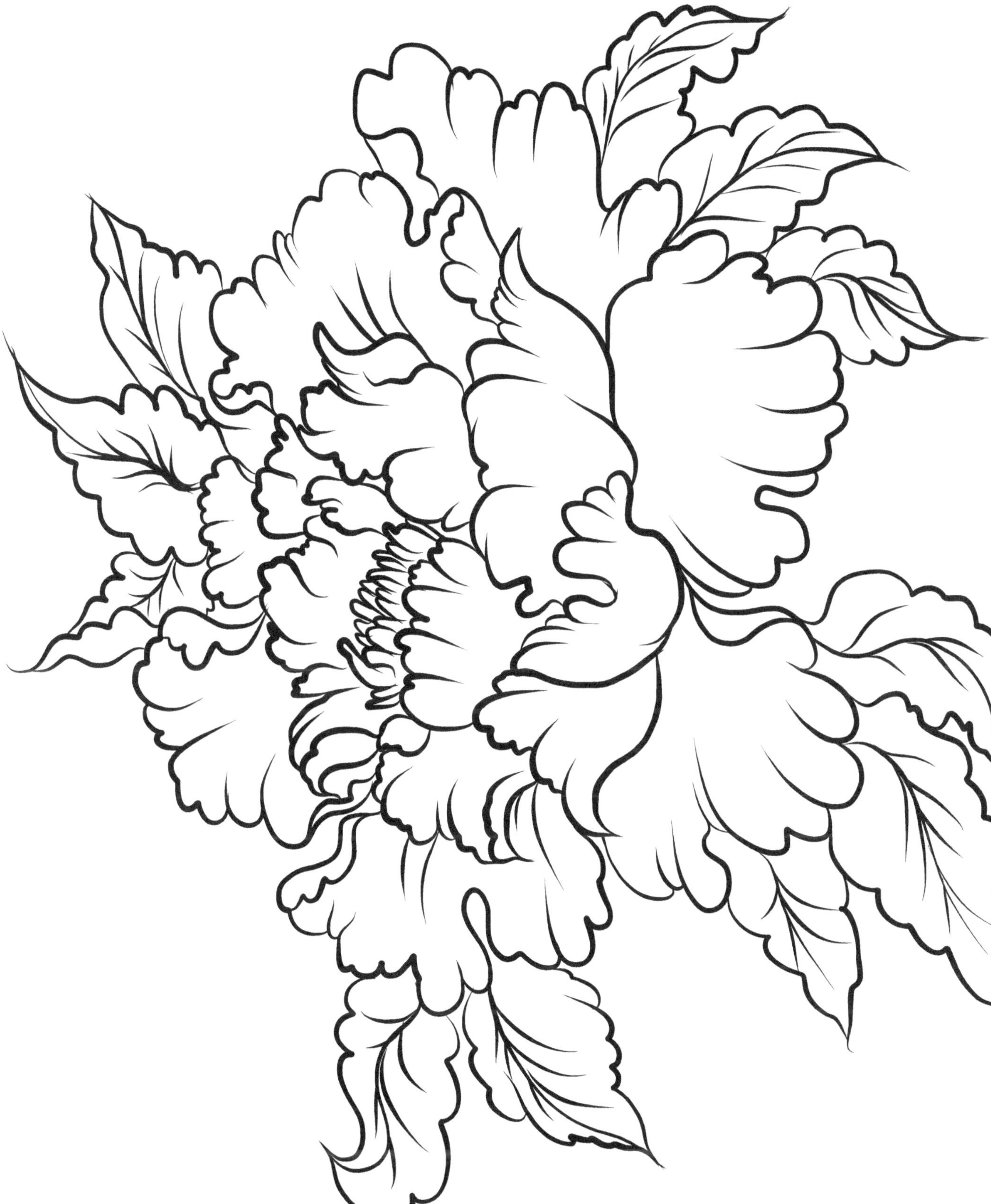

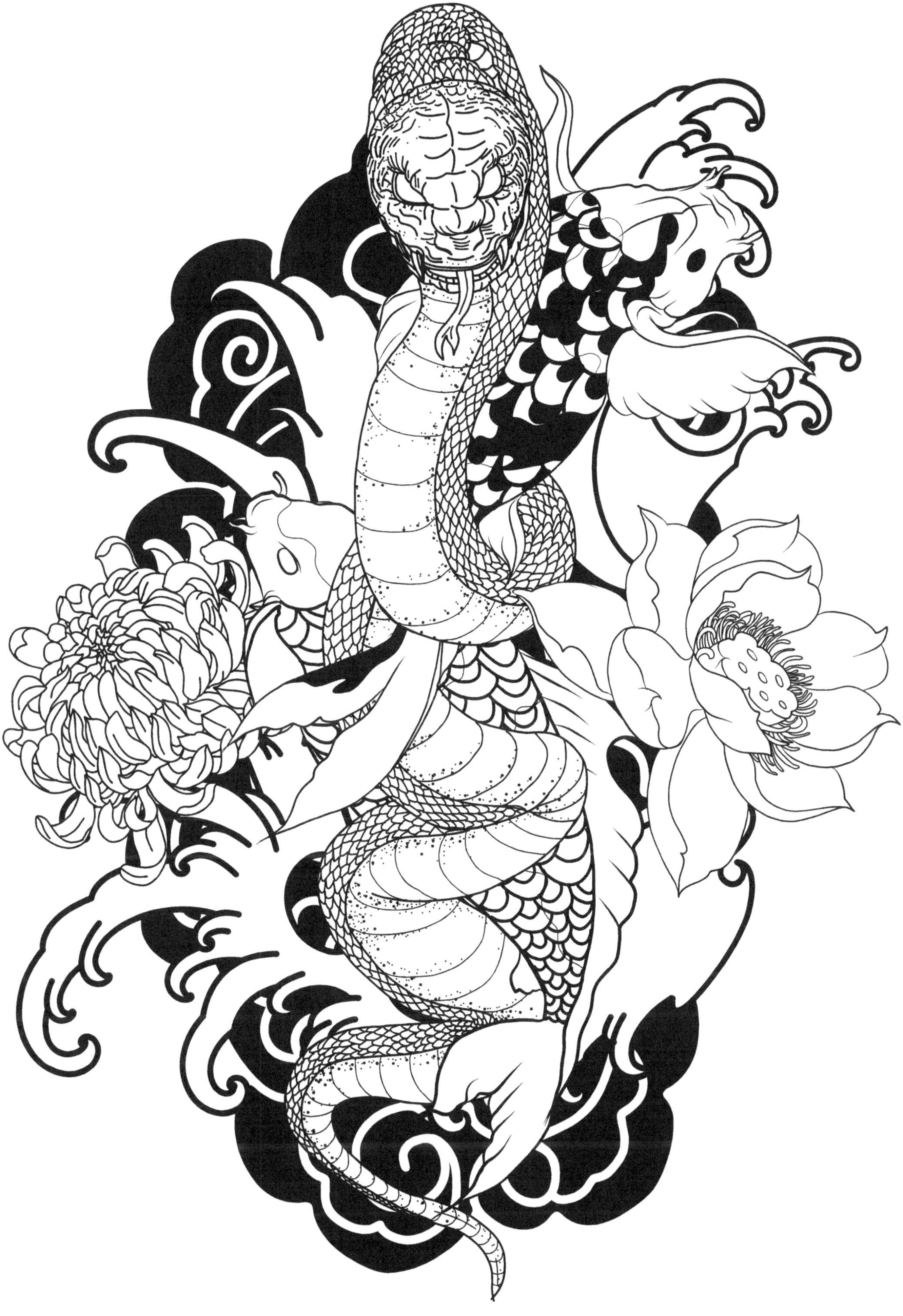

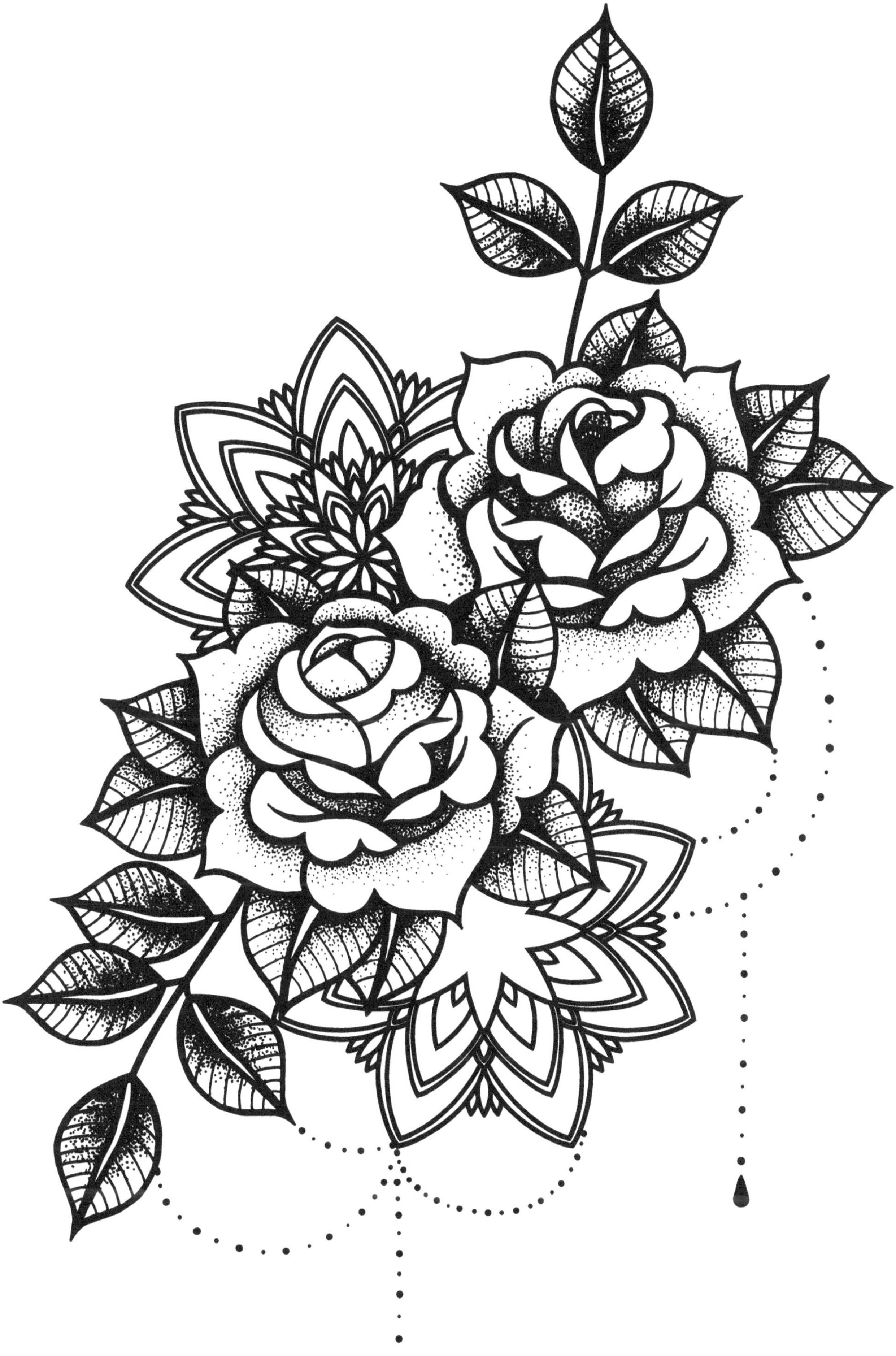

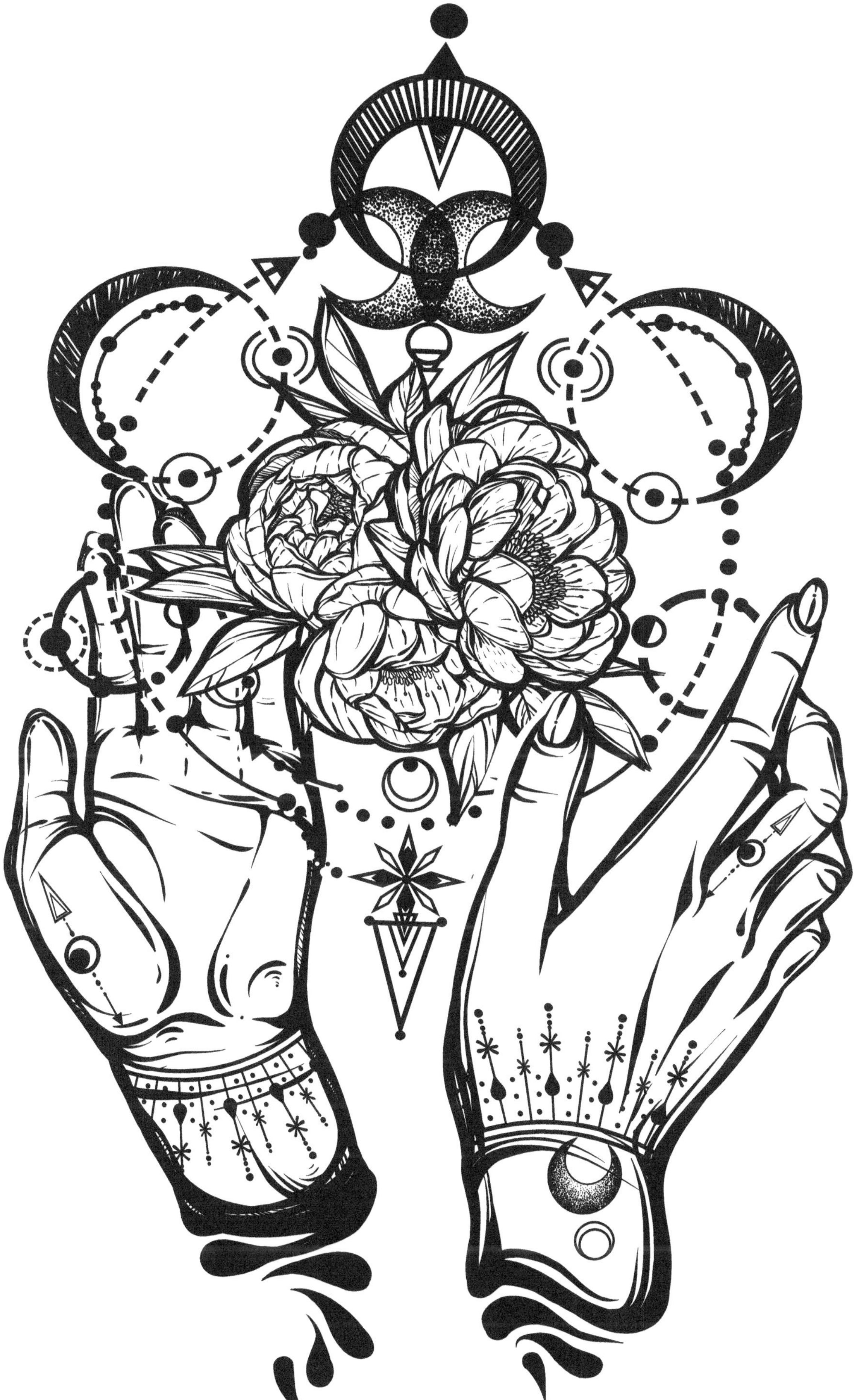

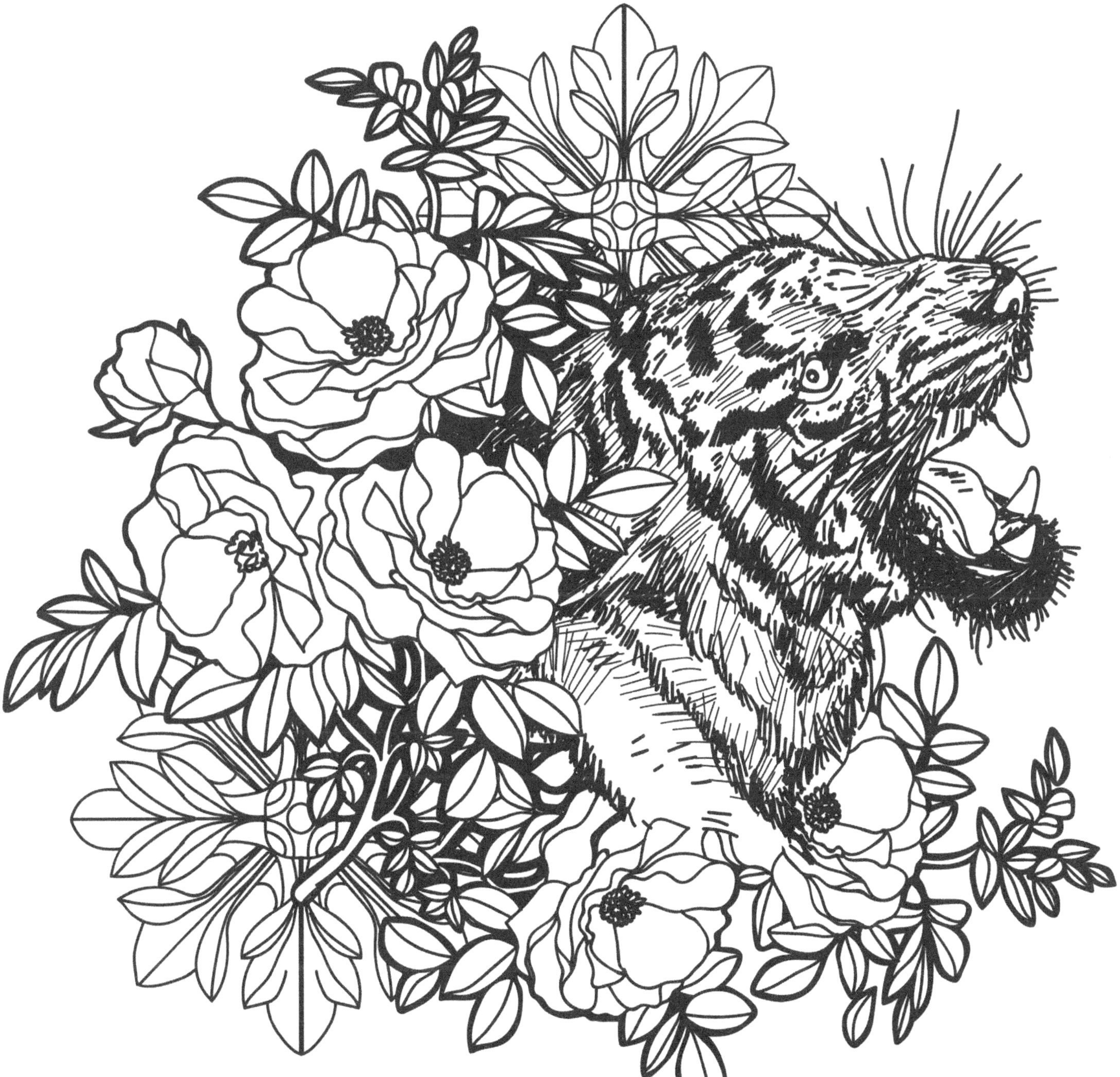

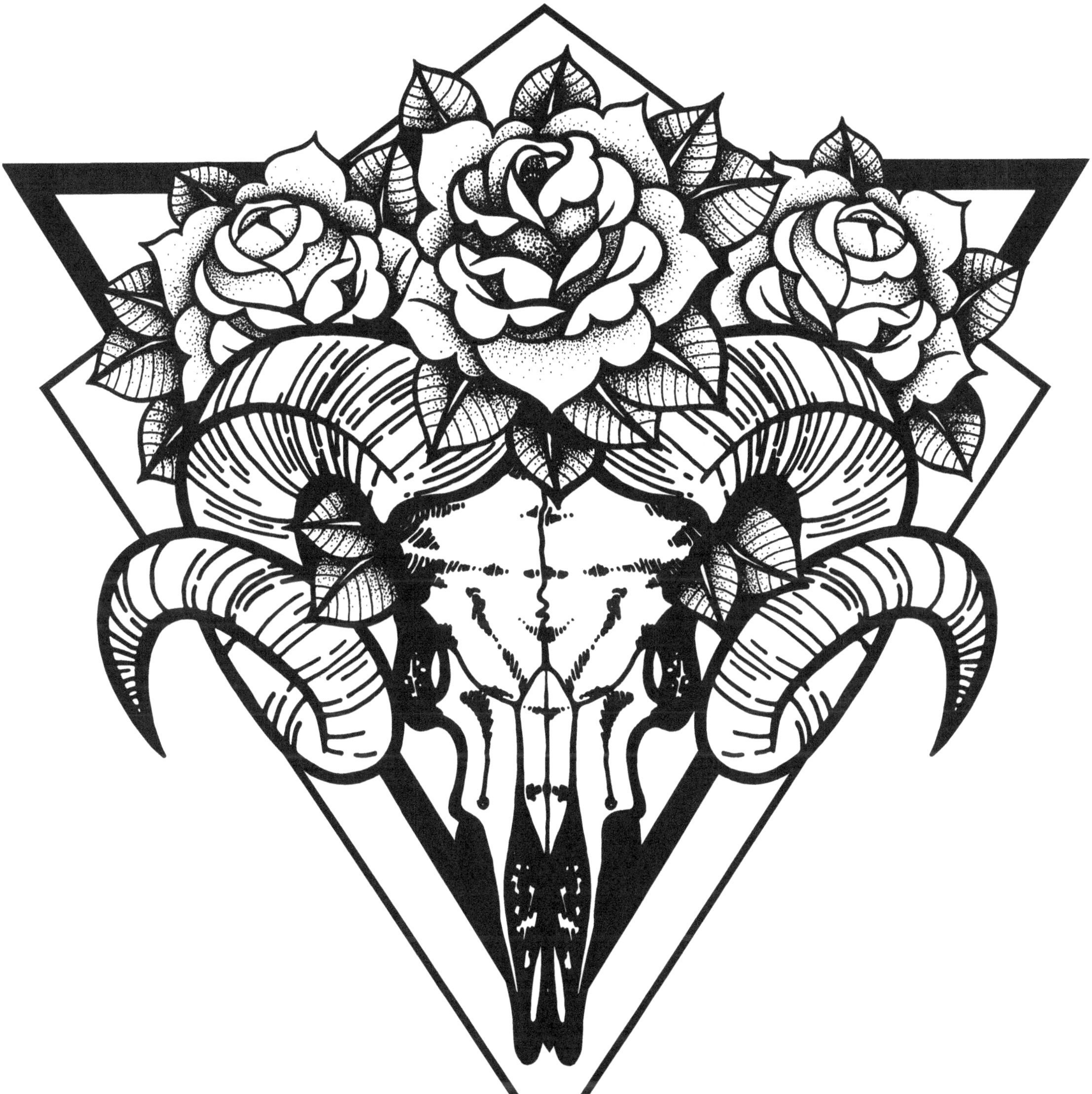

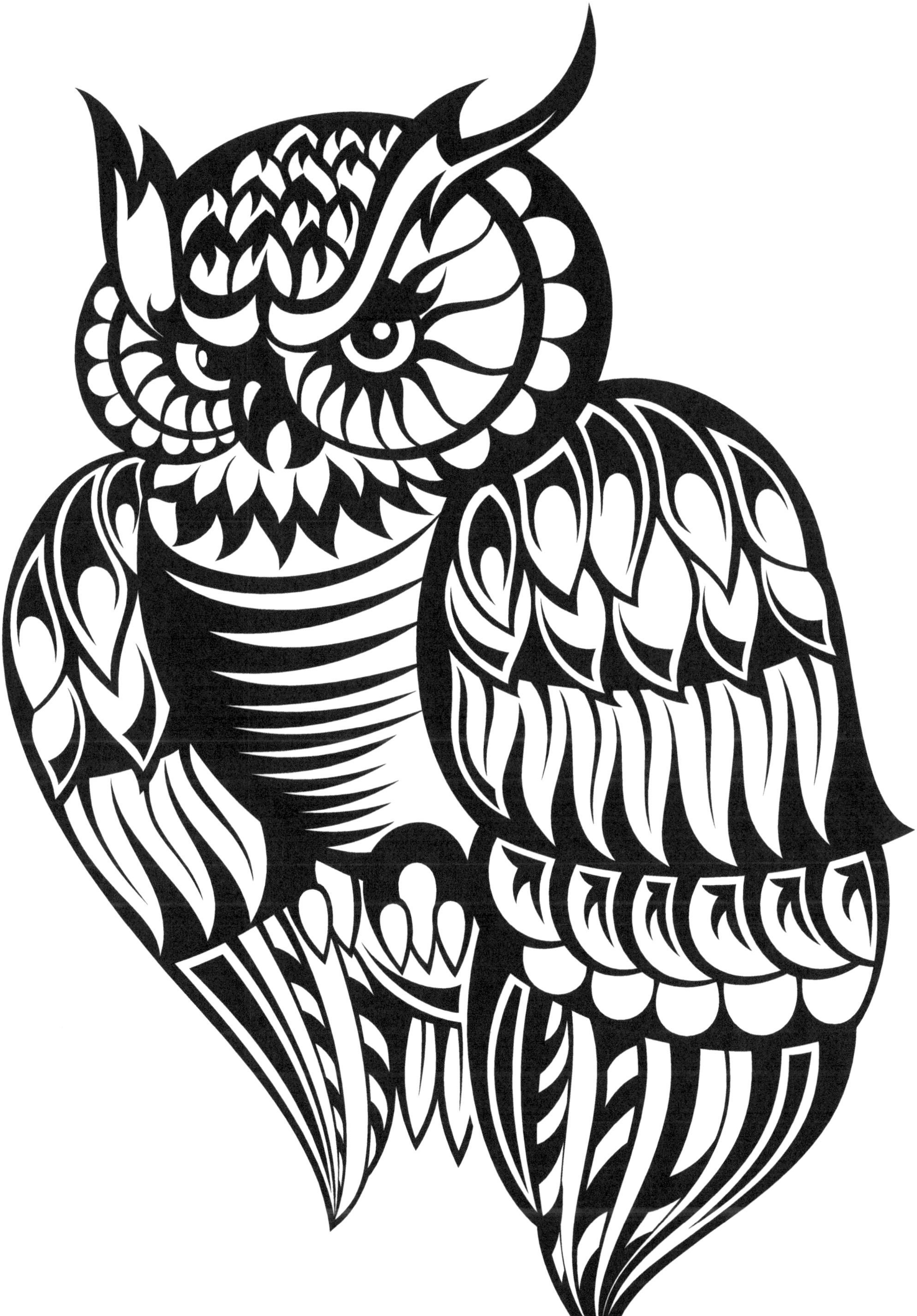

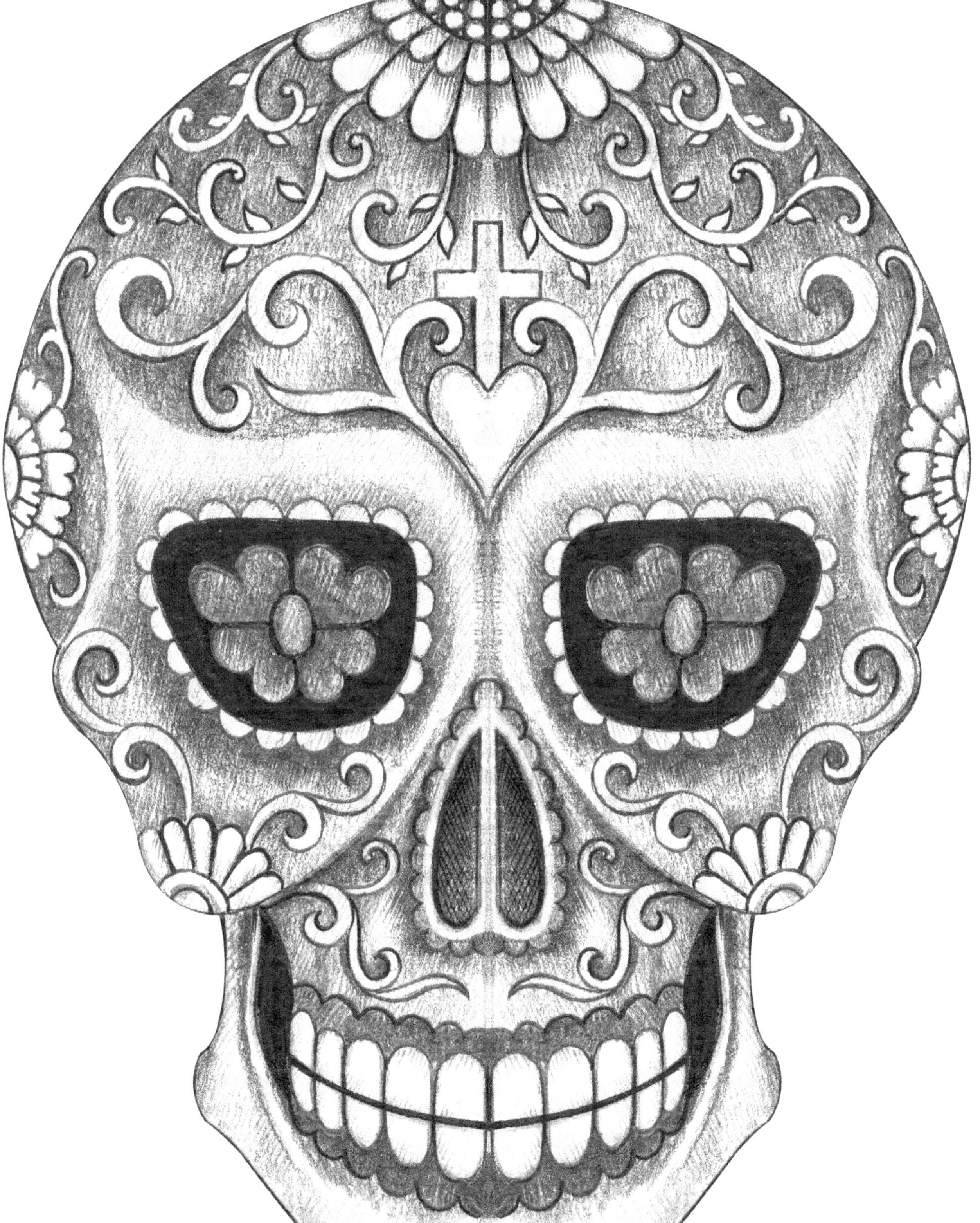

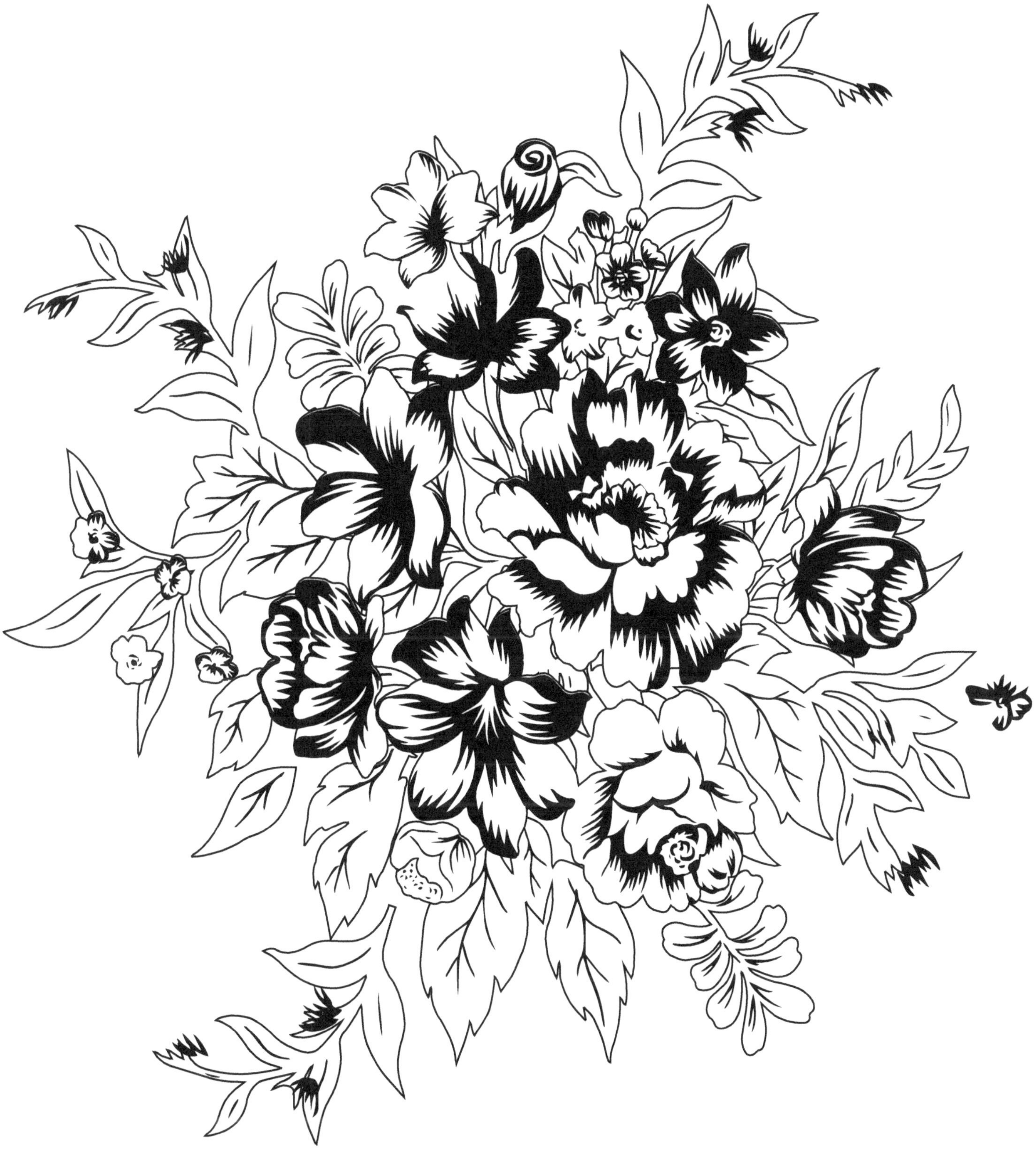

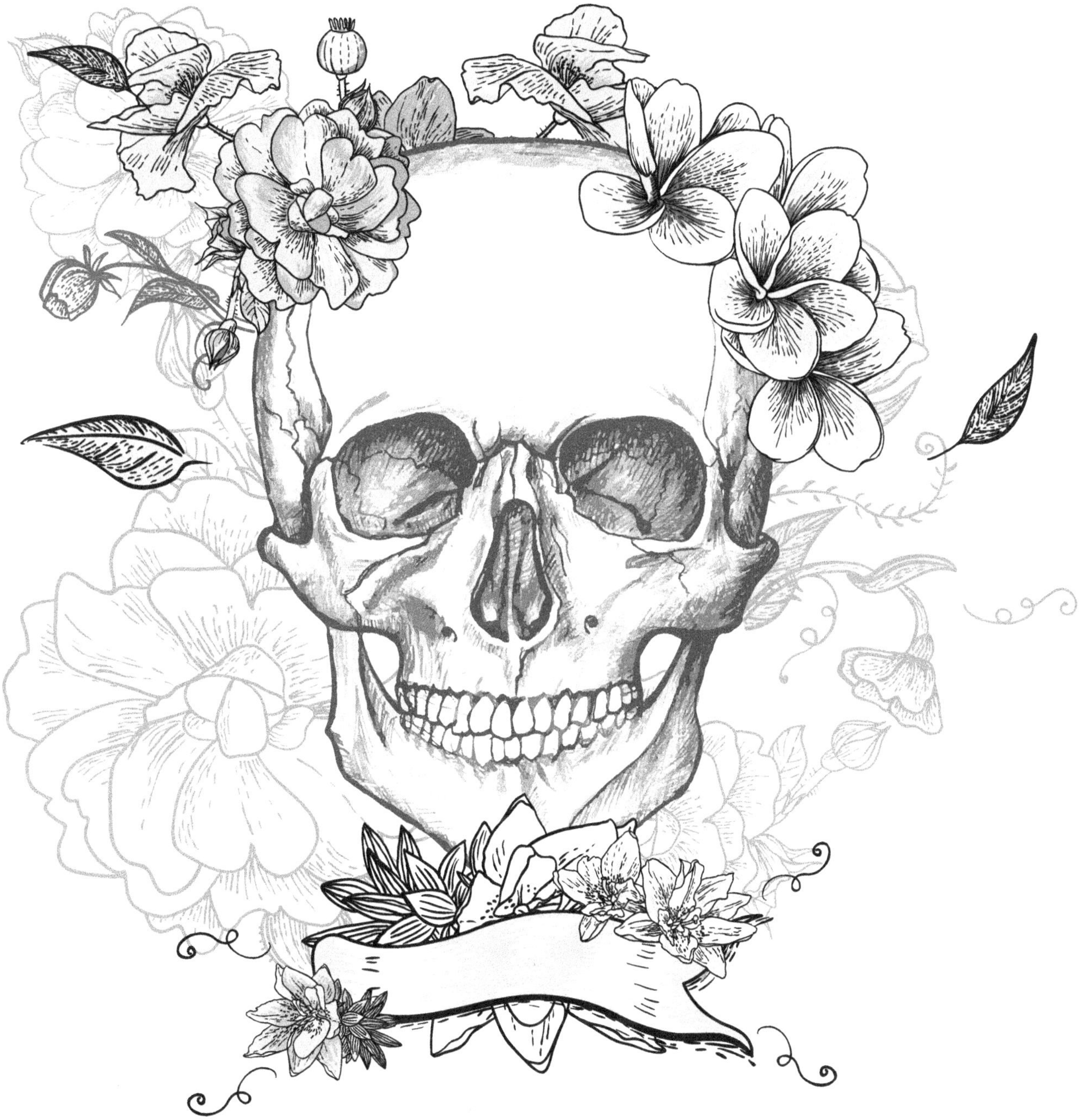

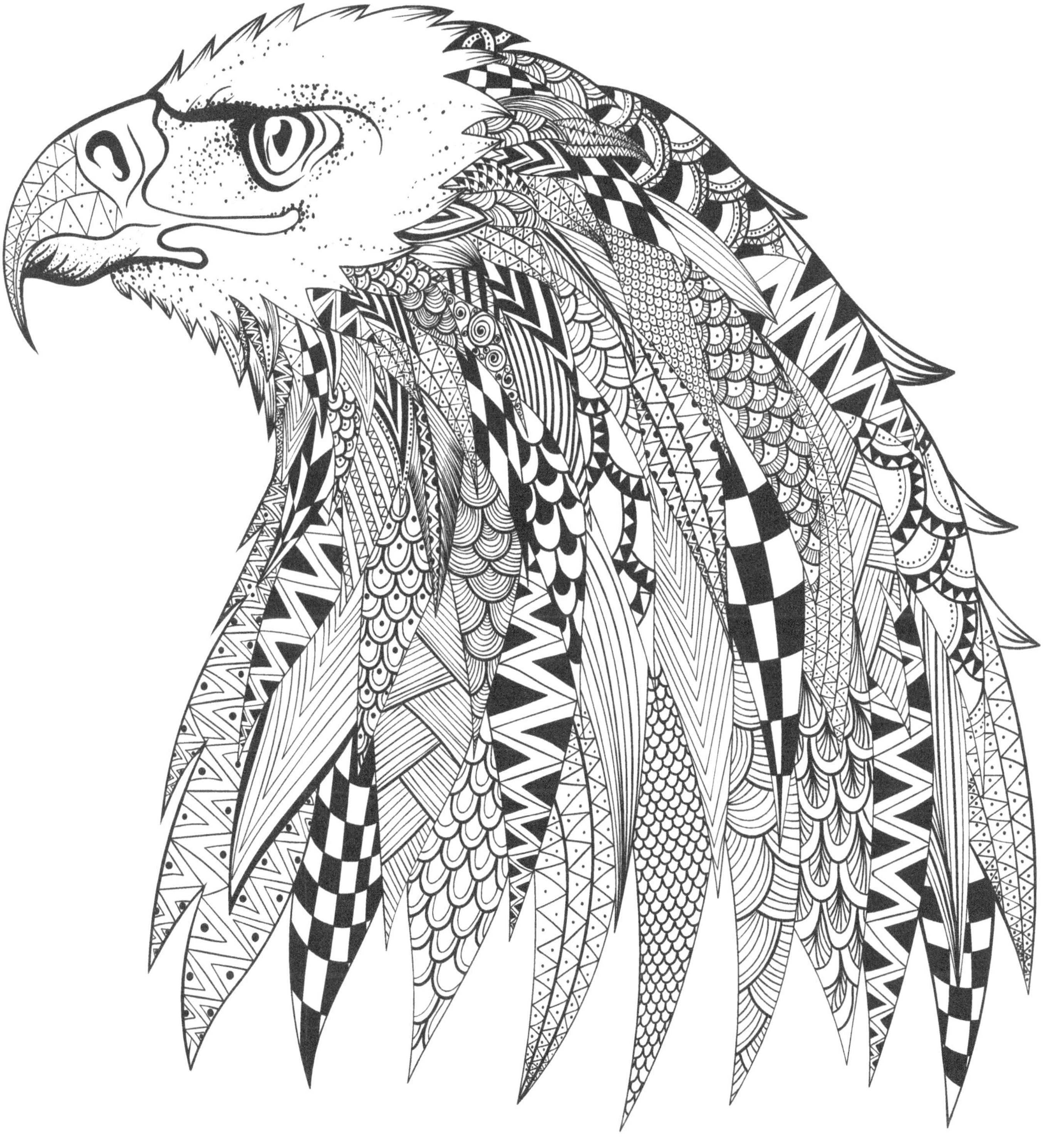

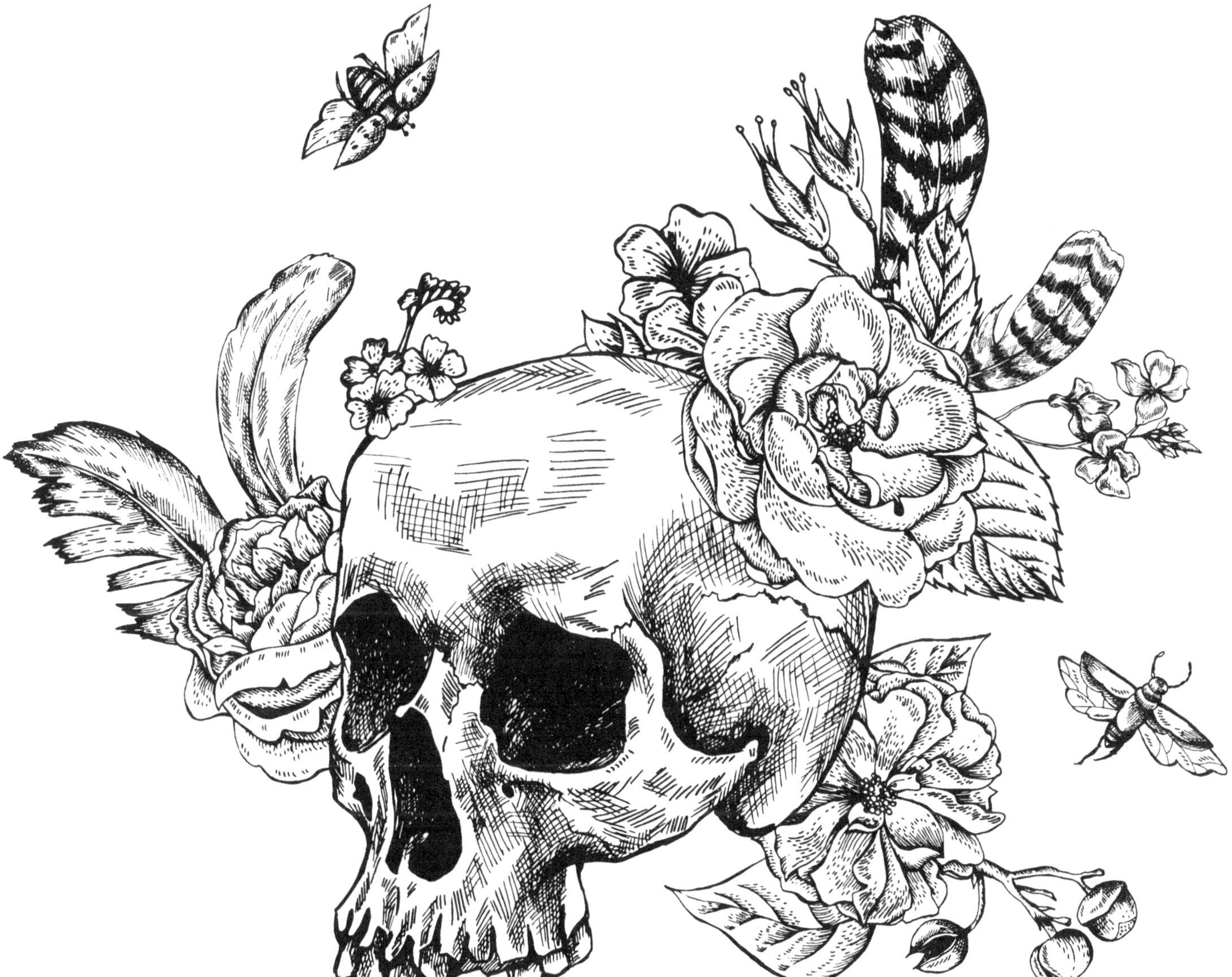

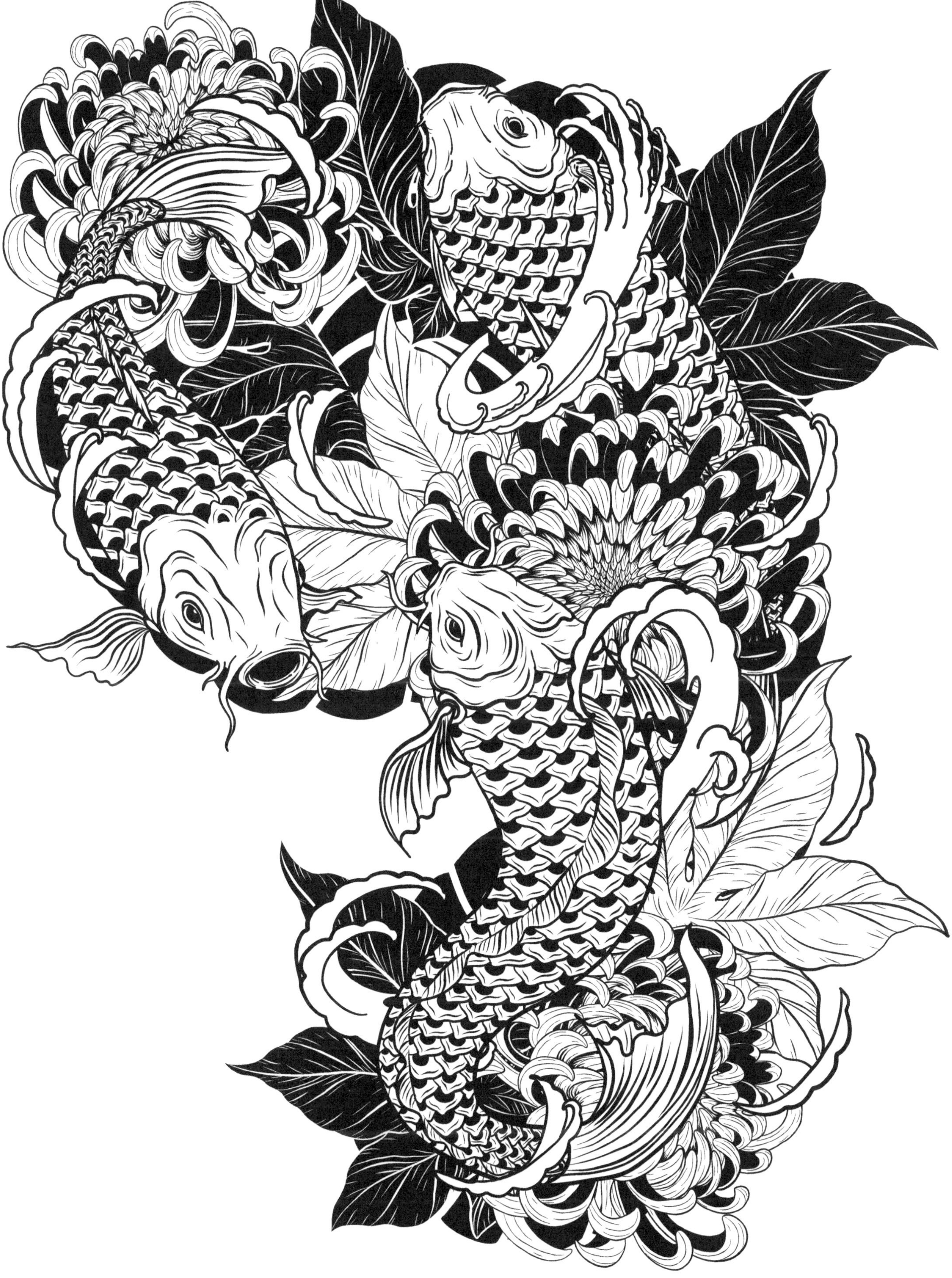

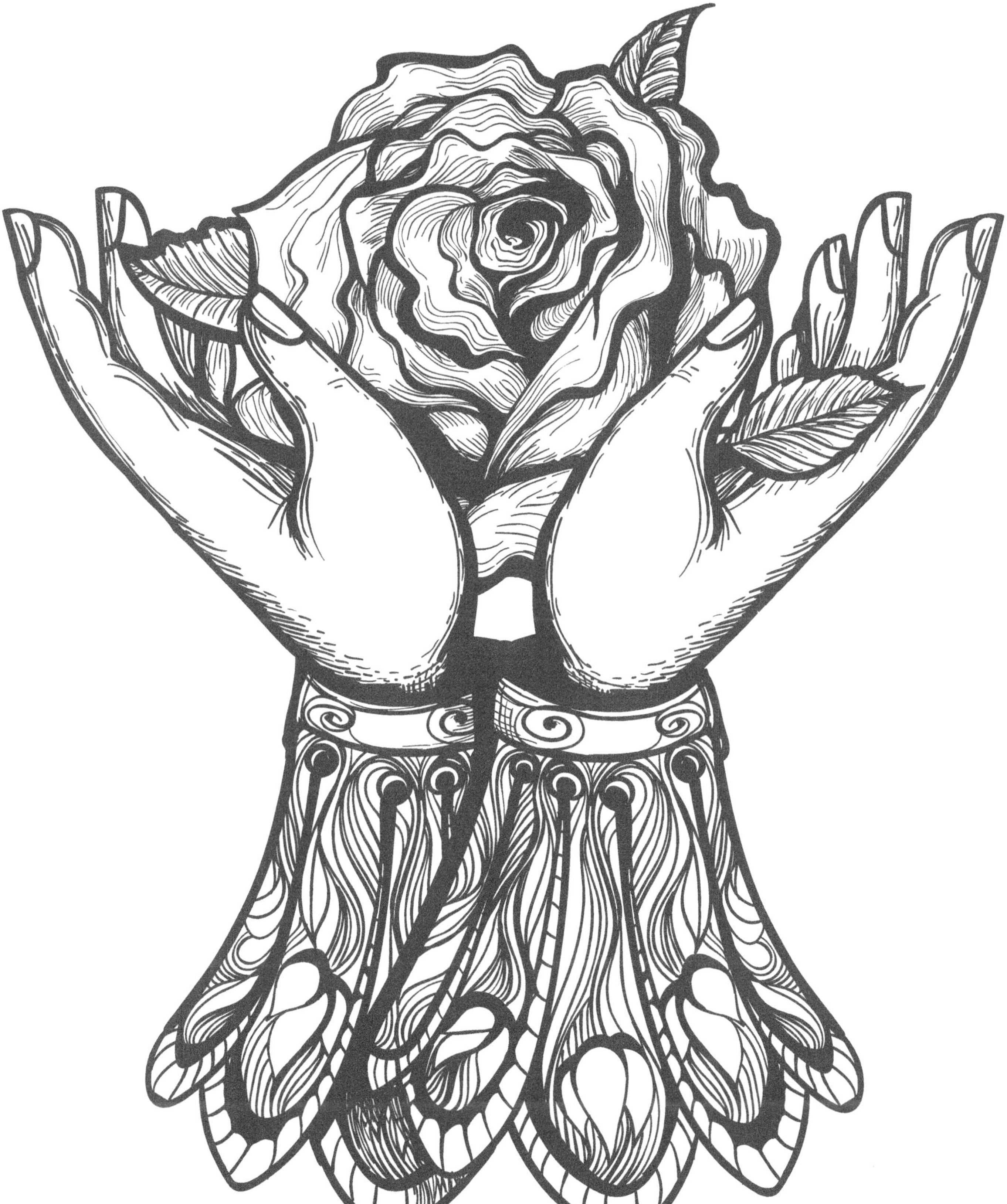

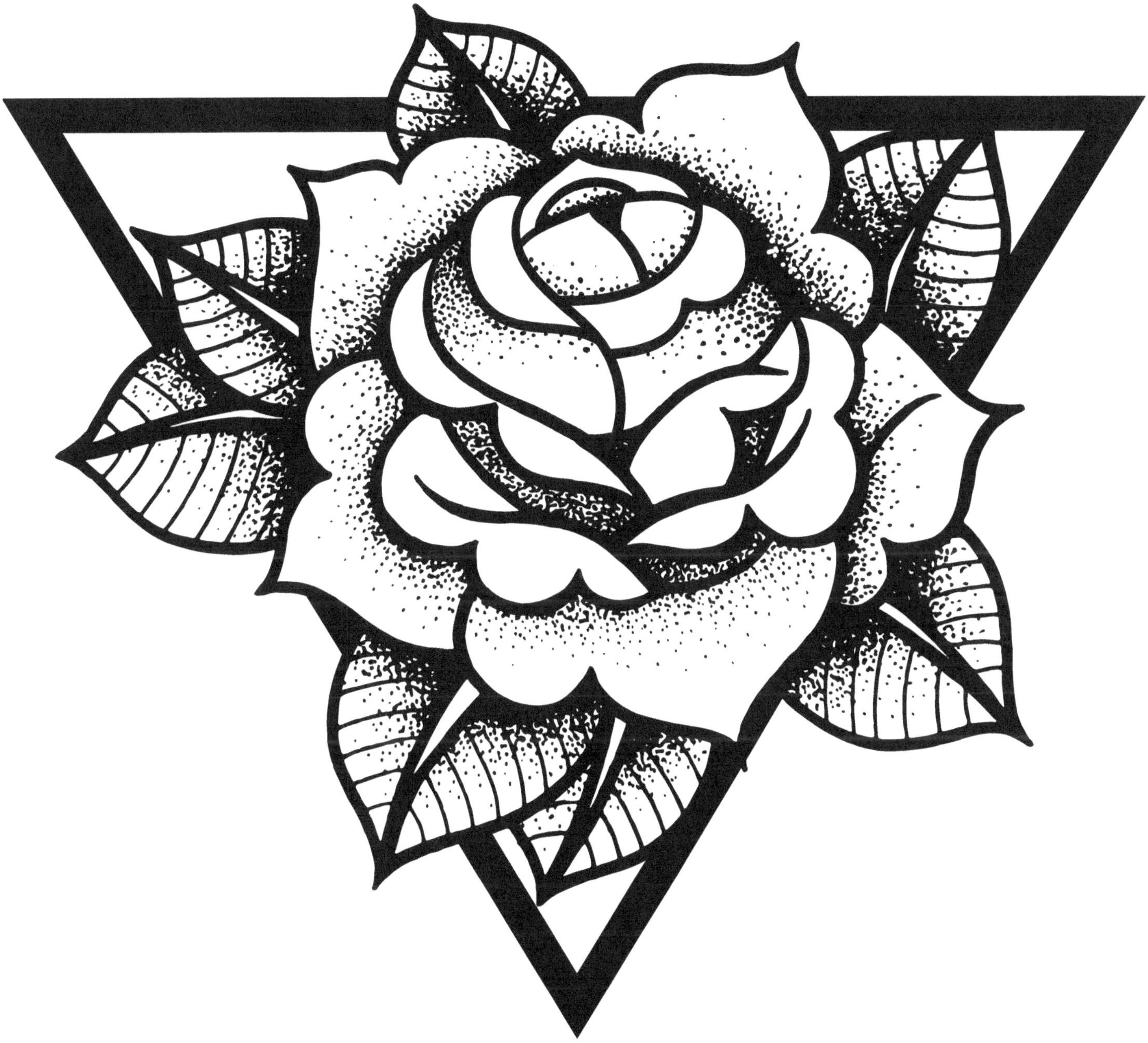

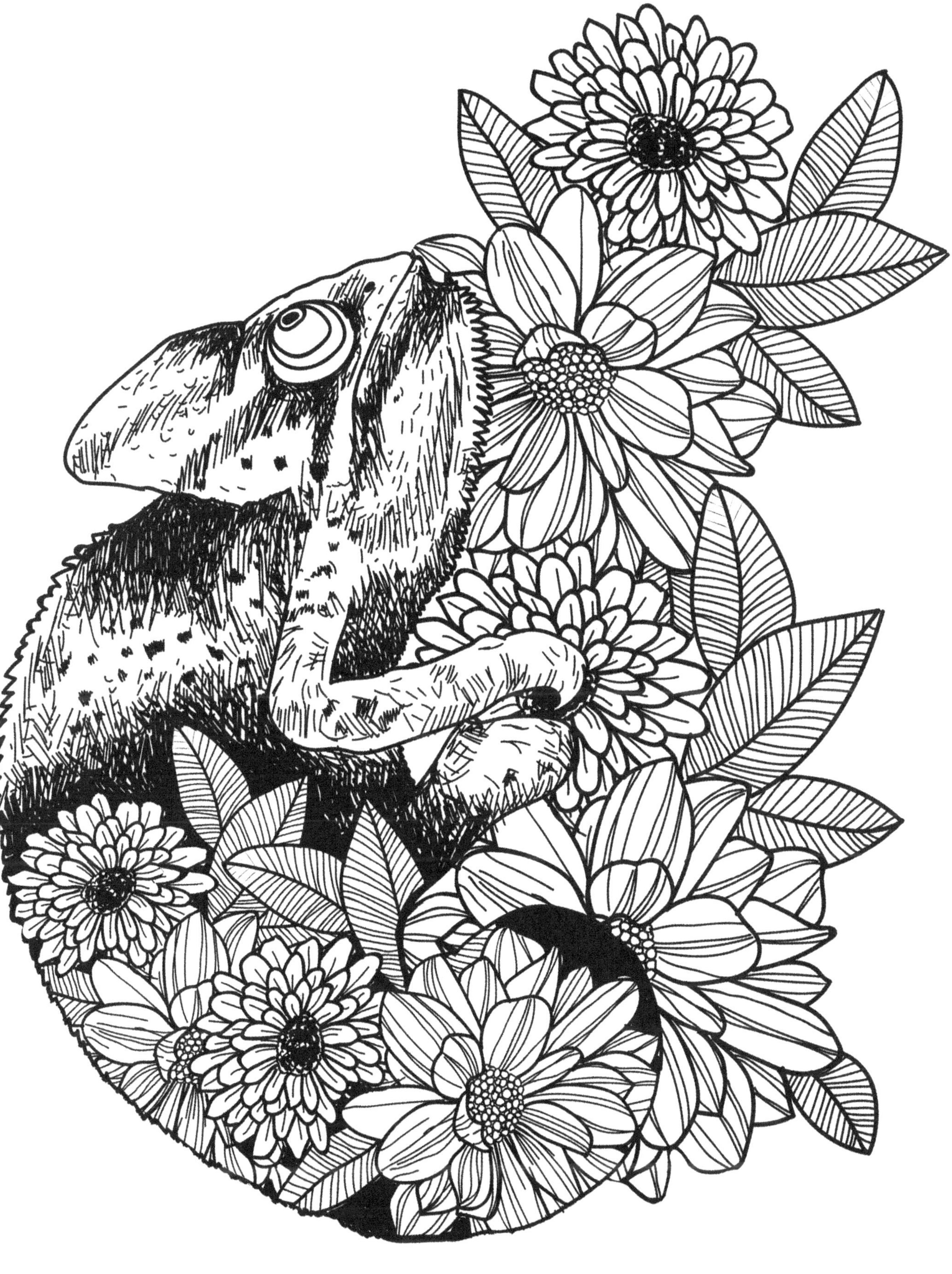

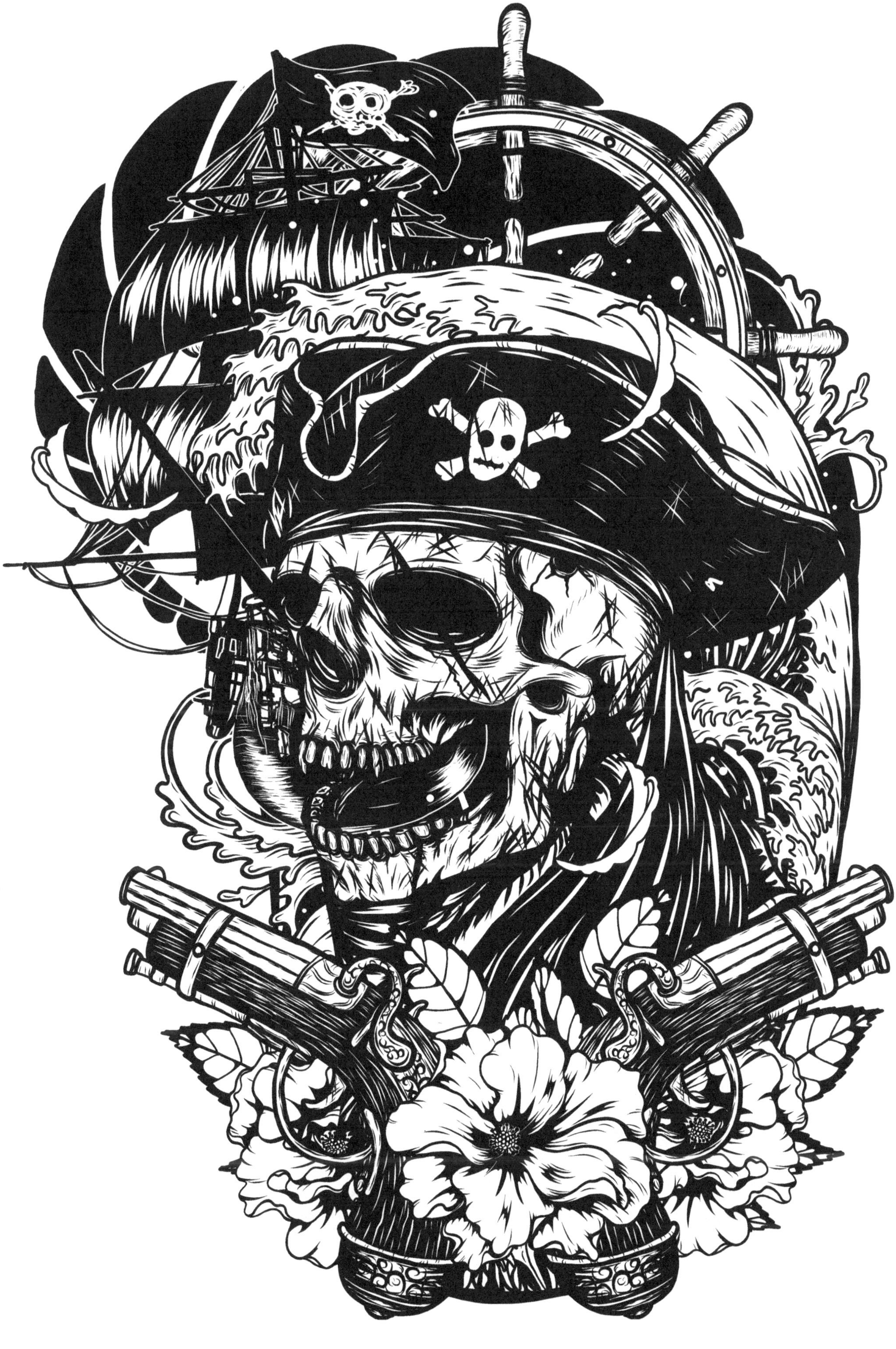

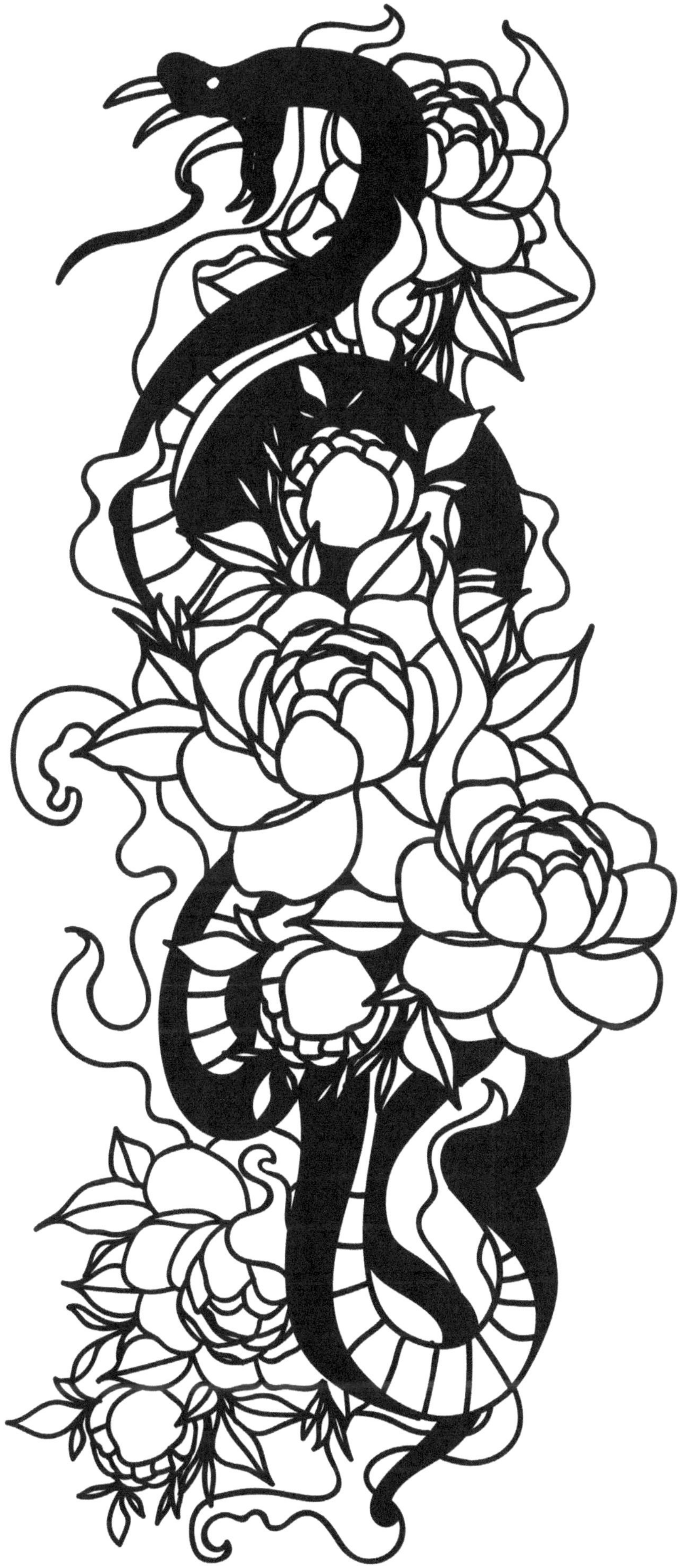

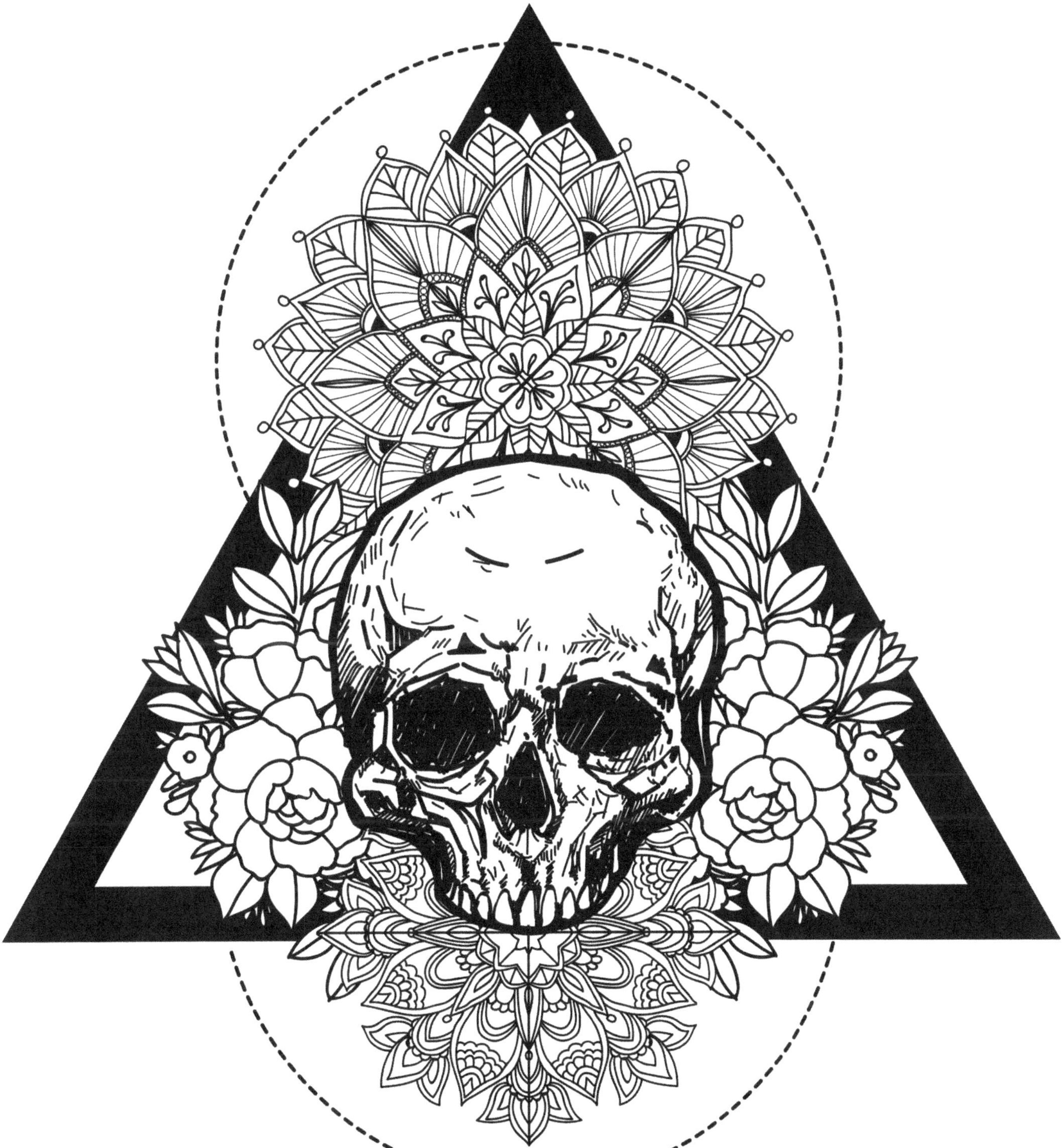

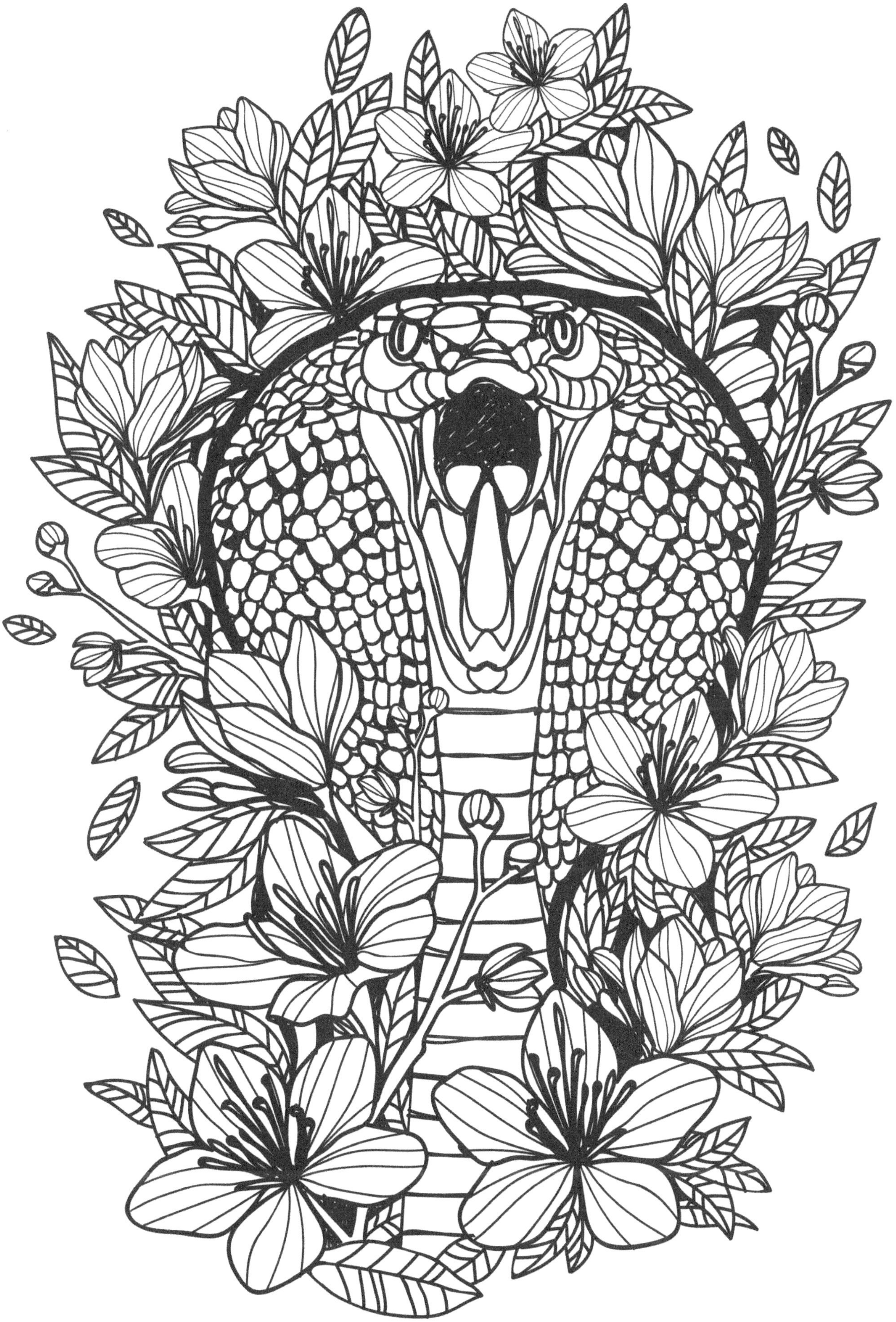

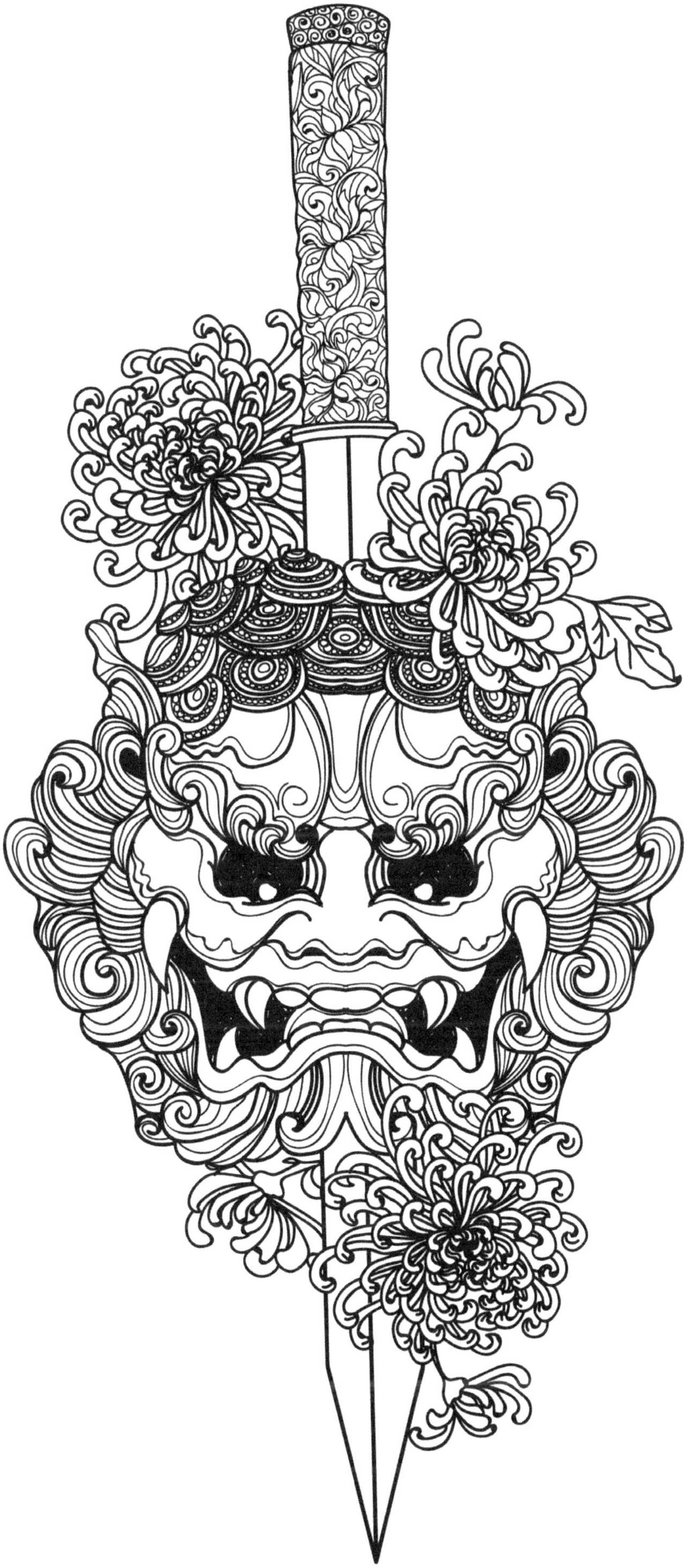

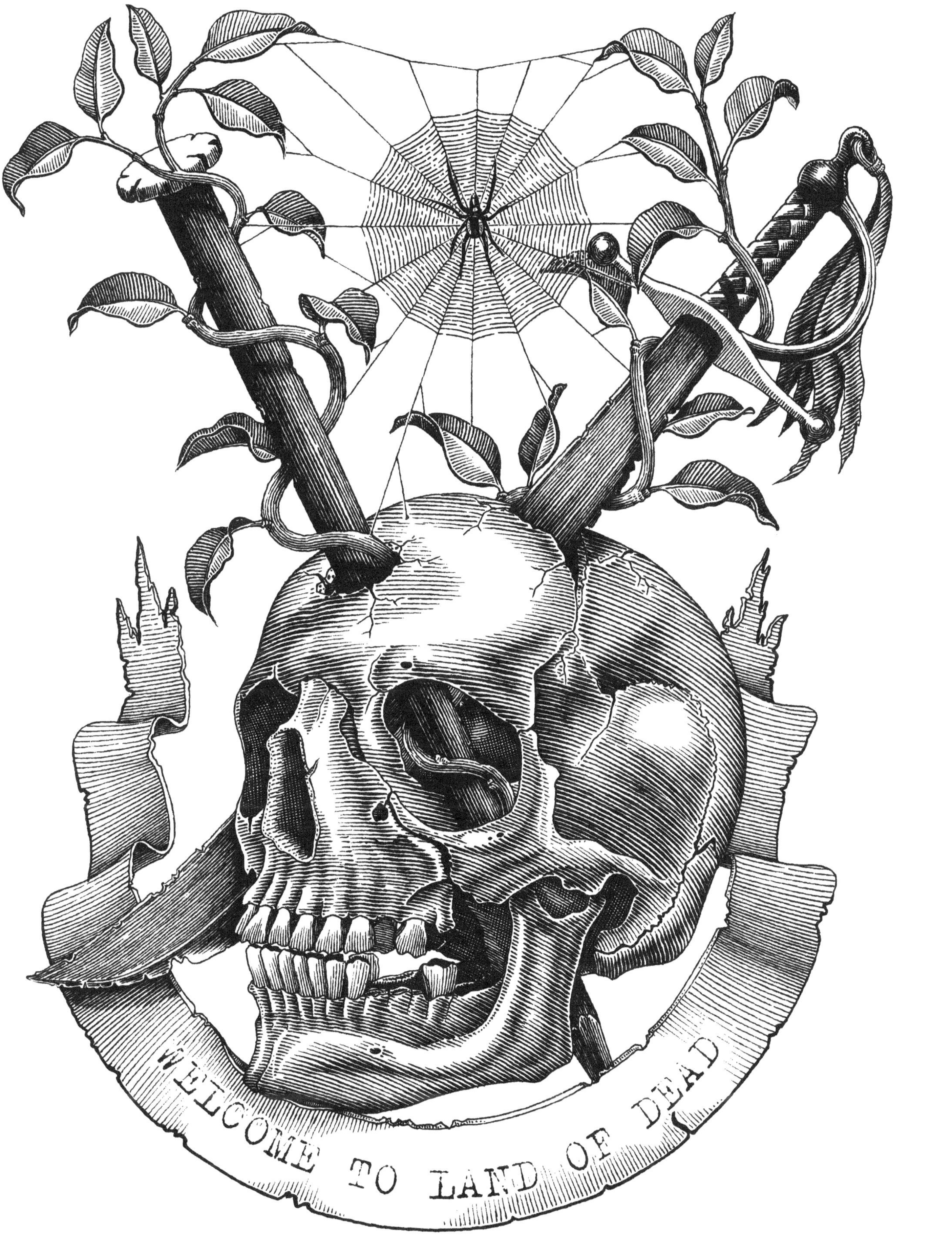
WELCOME TO LAND OF DEAD

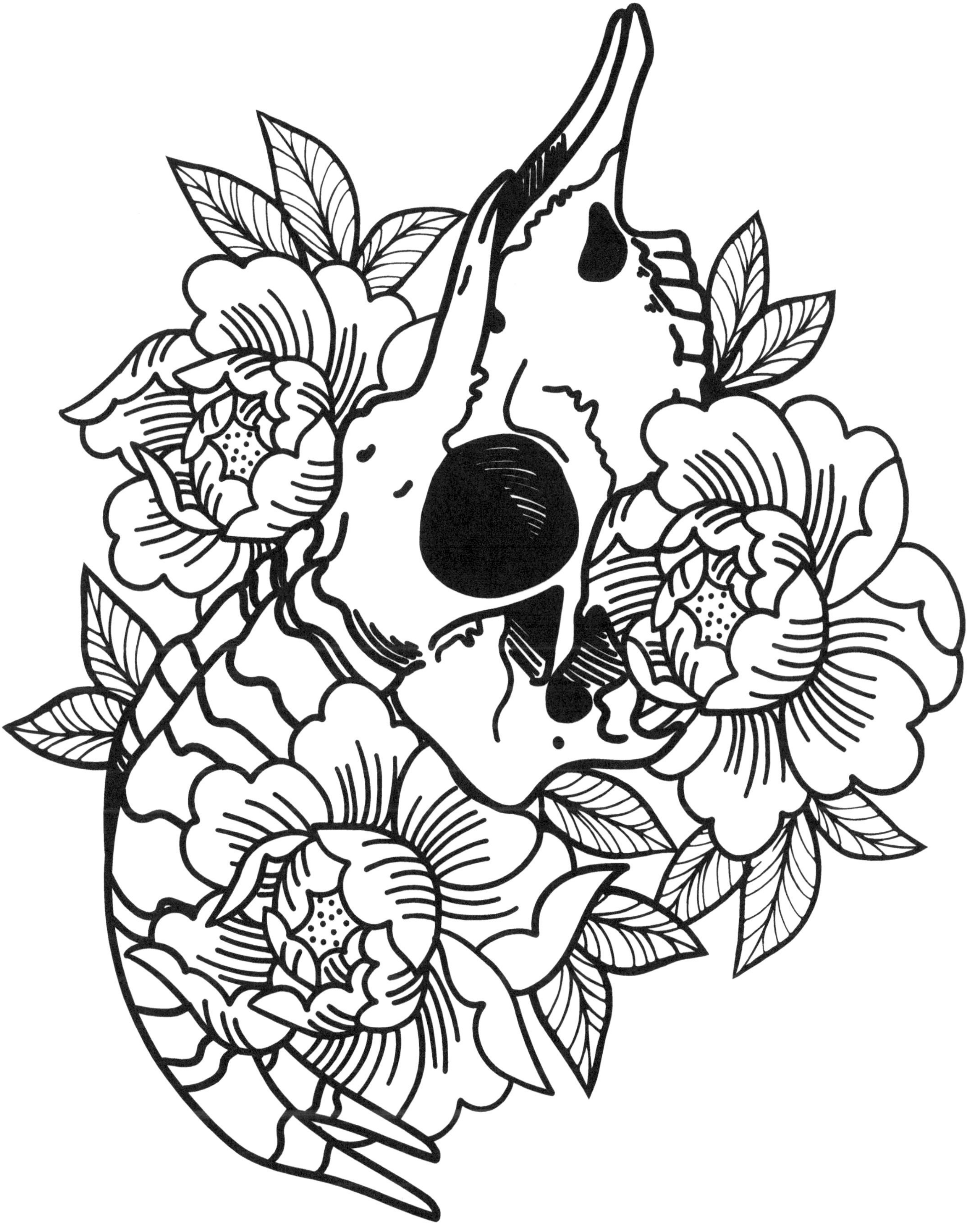

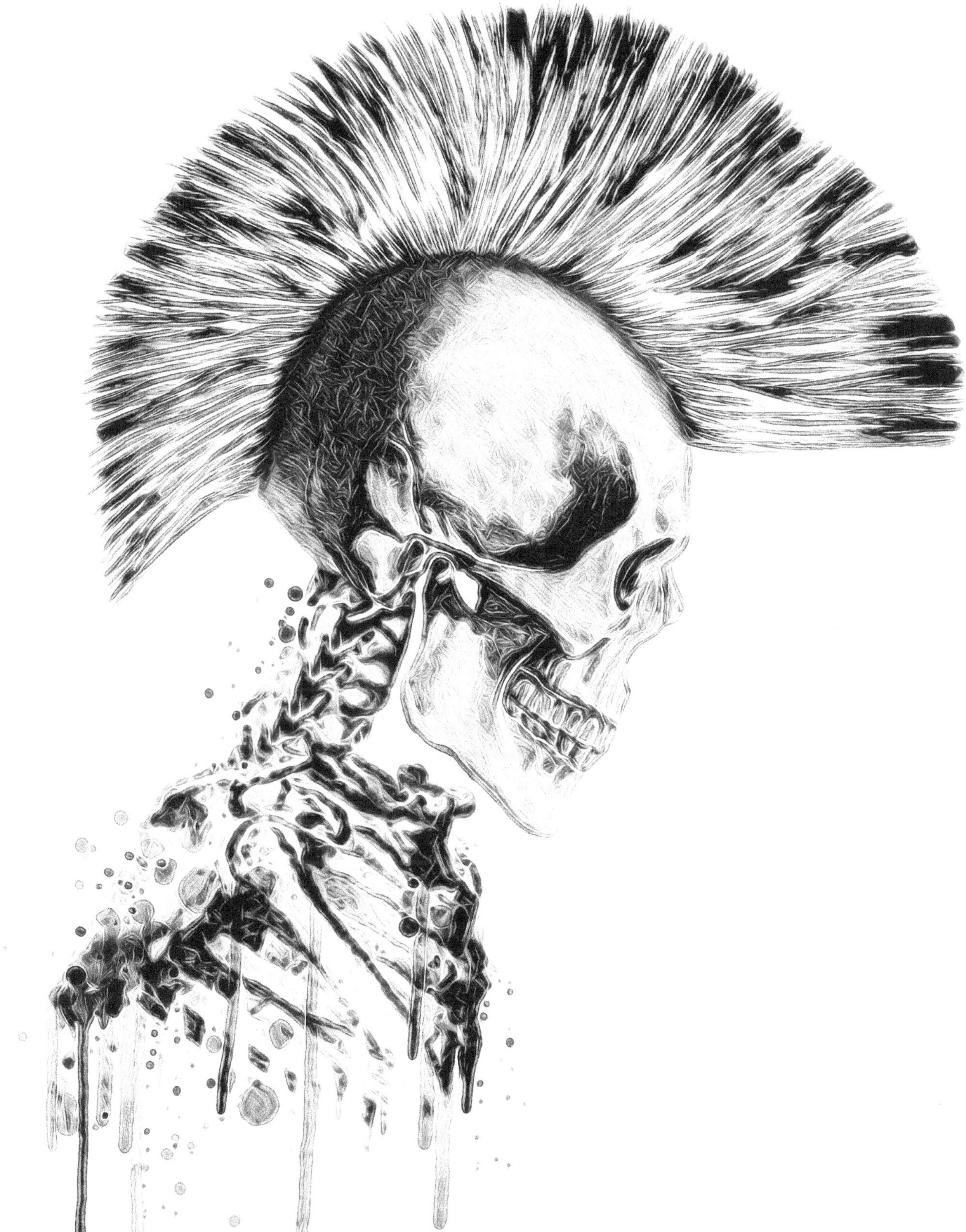

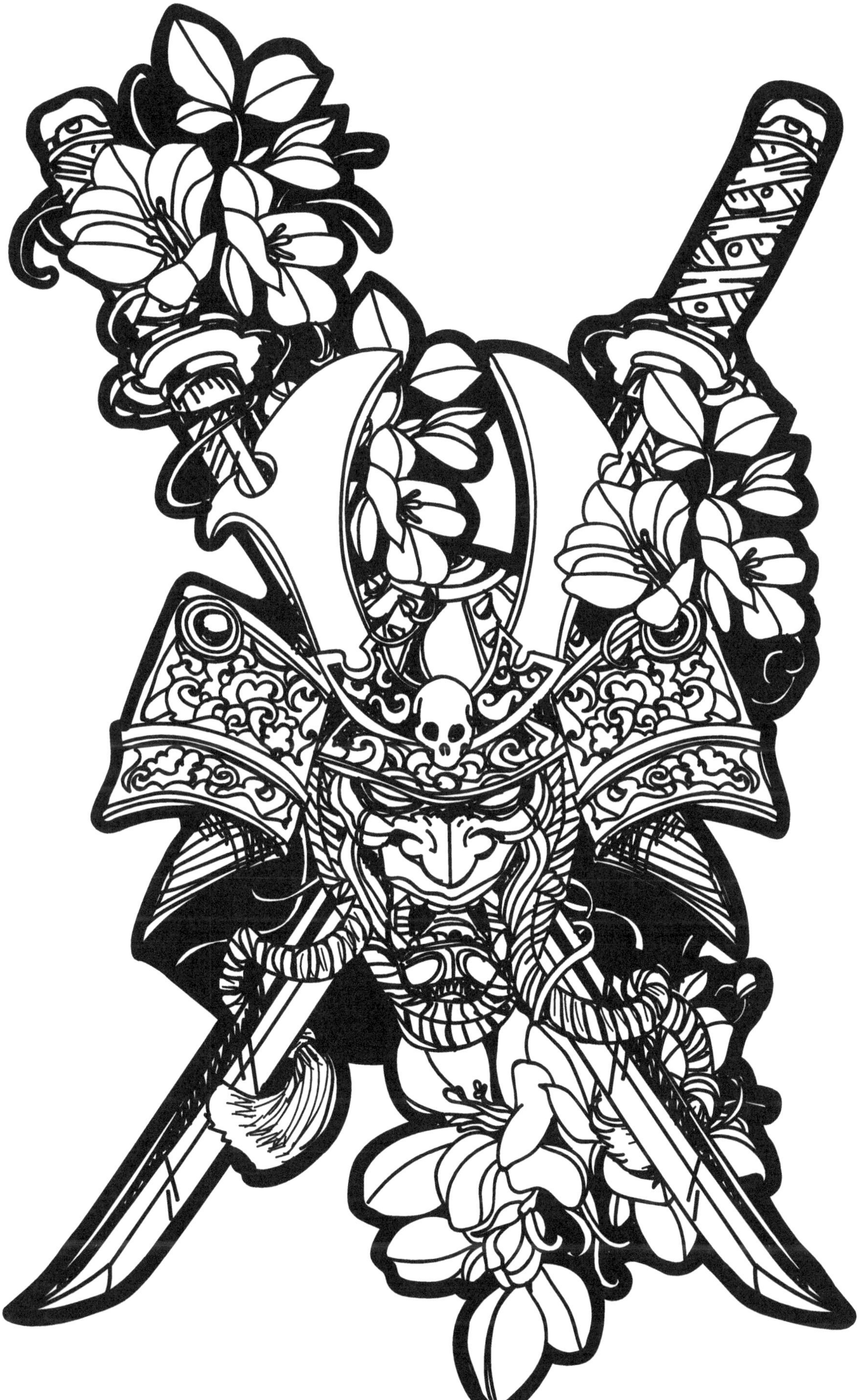

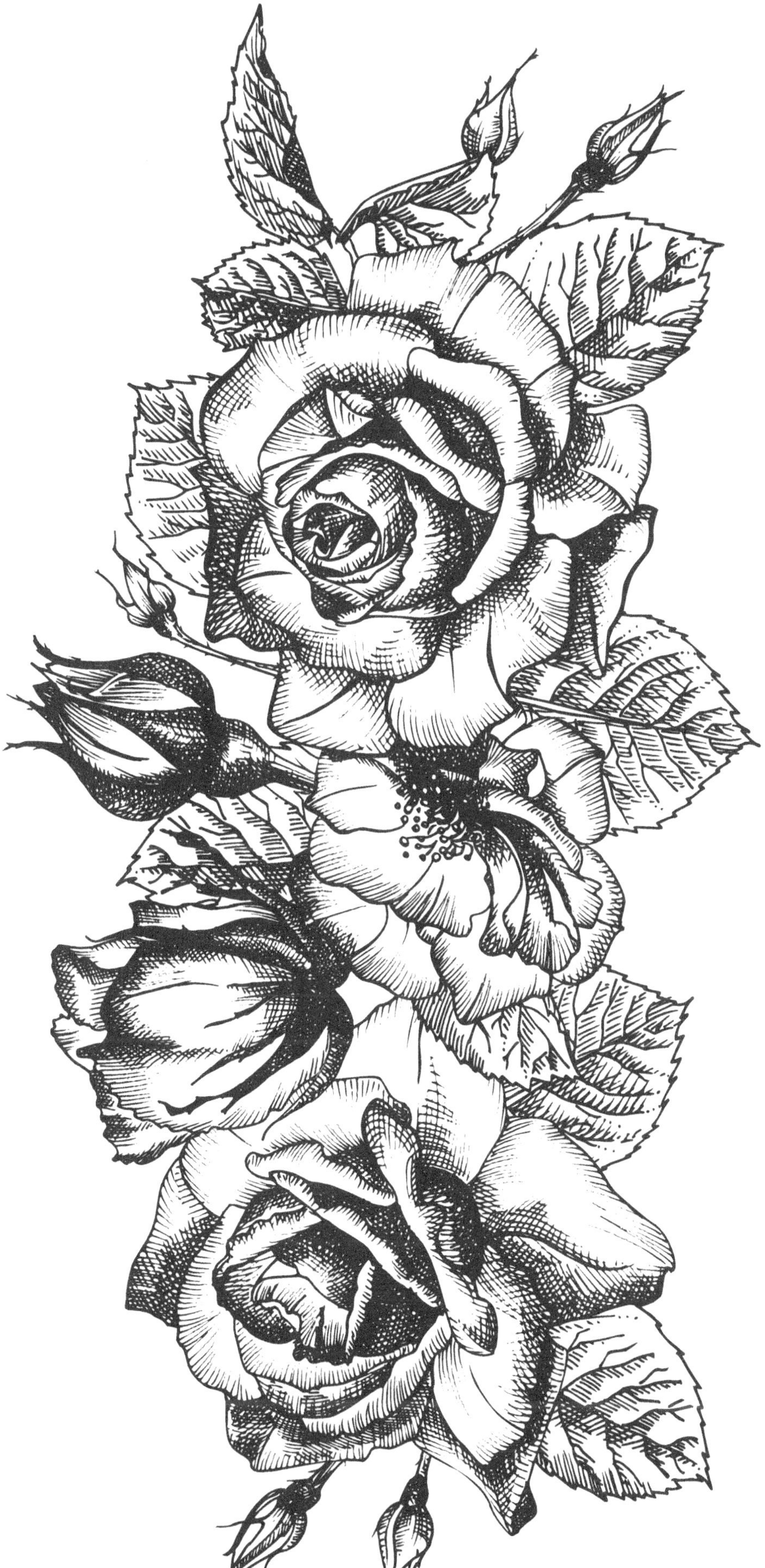

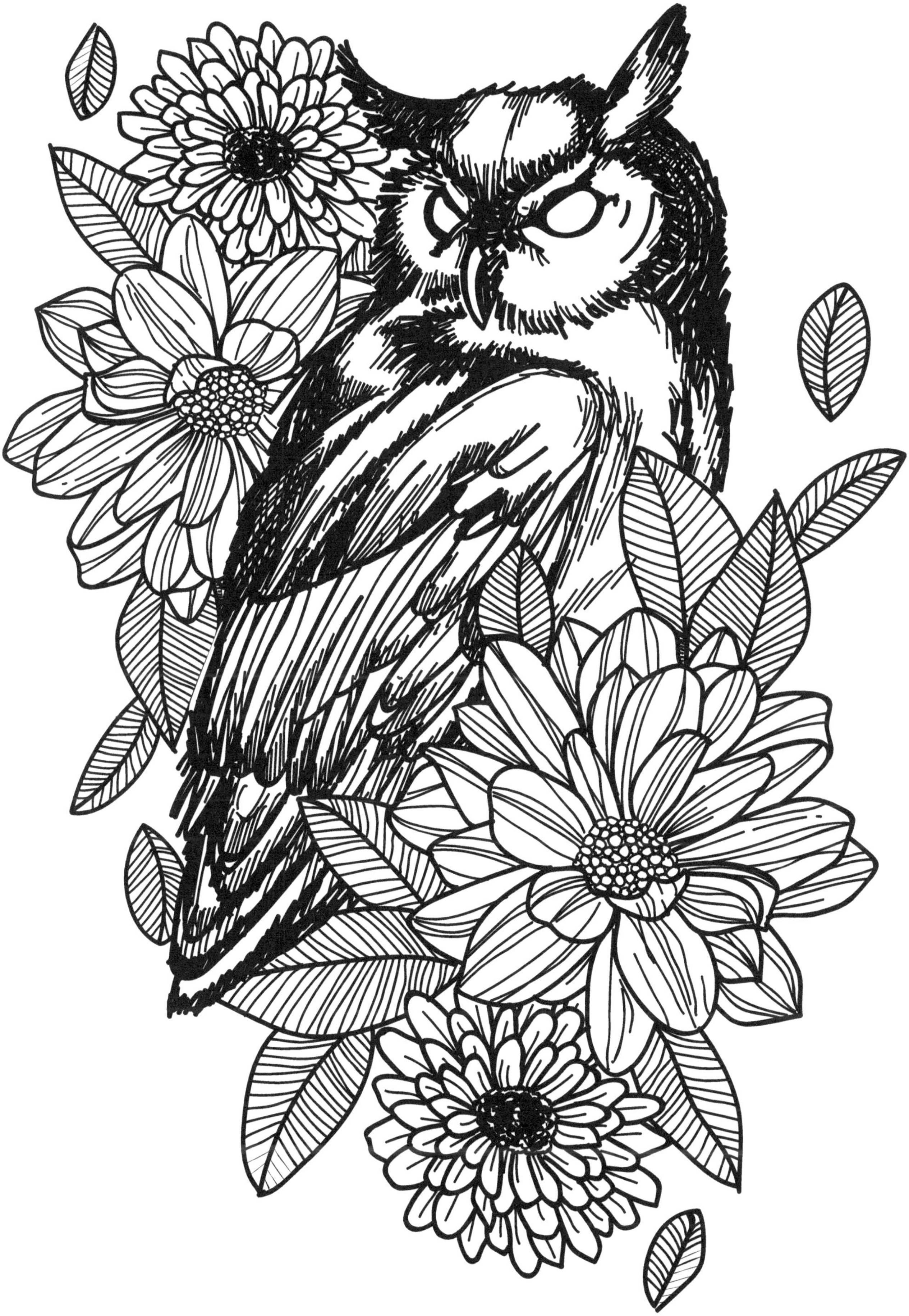

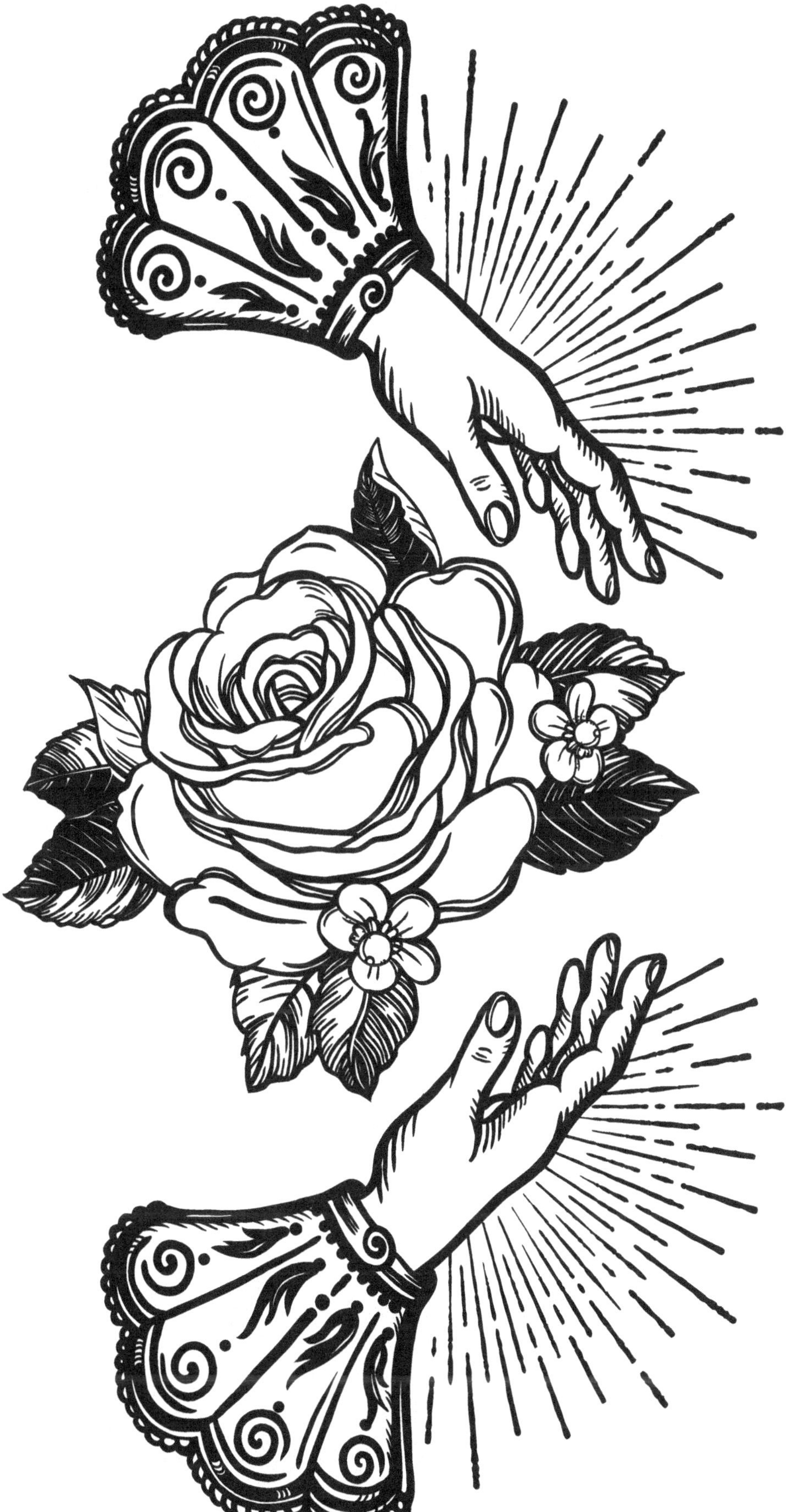

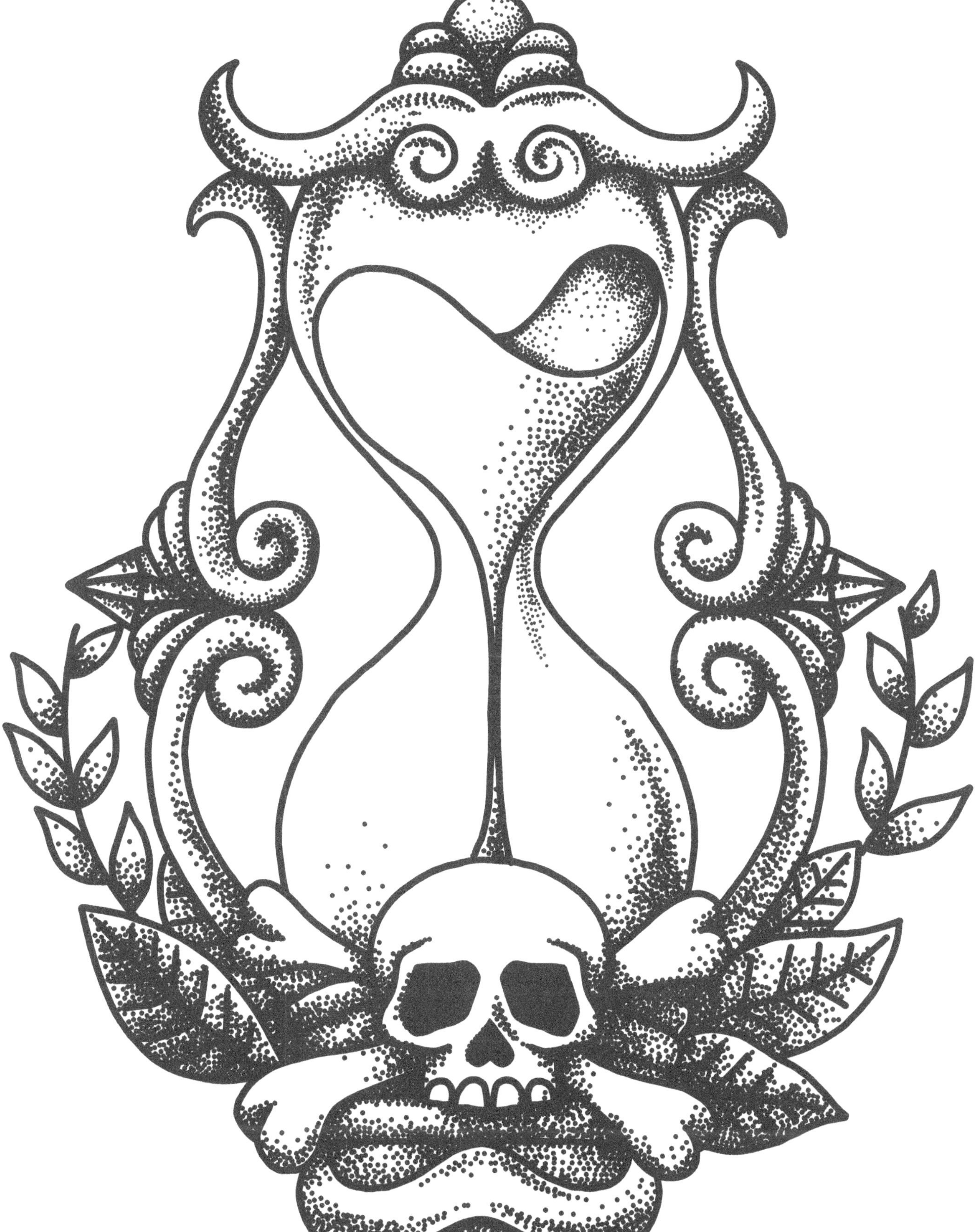

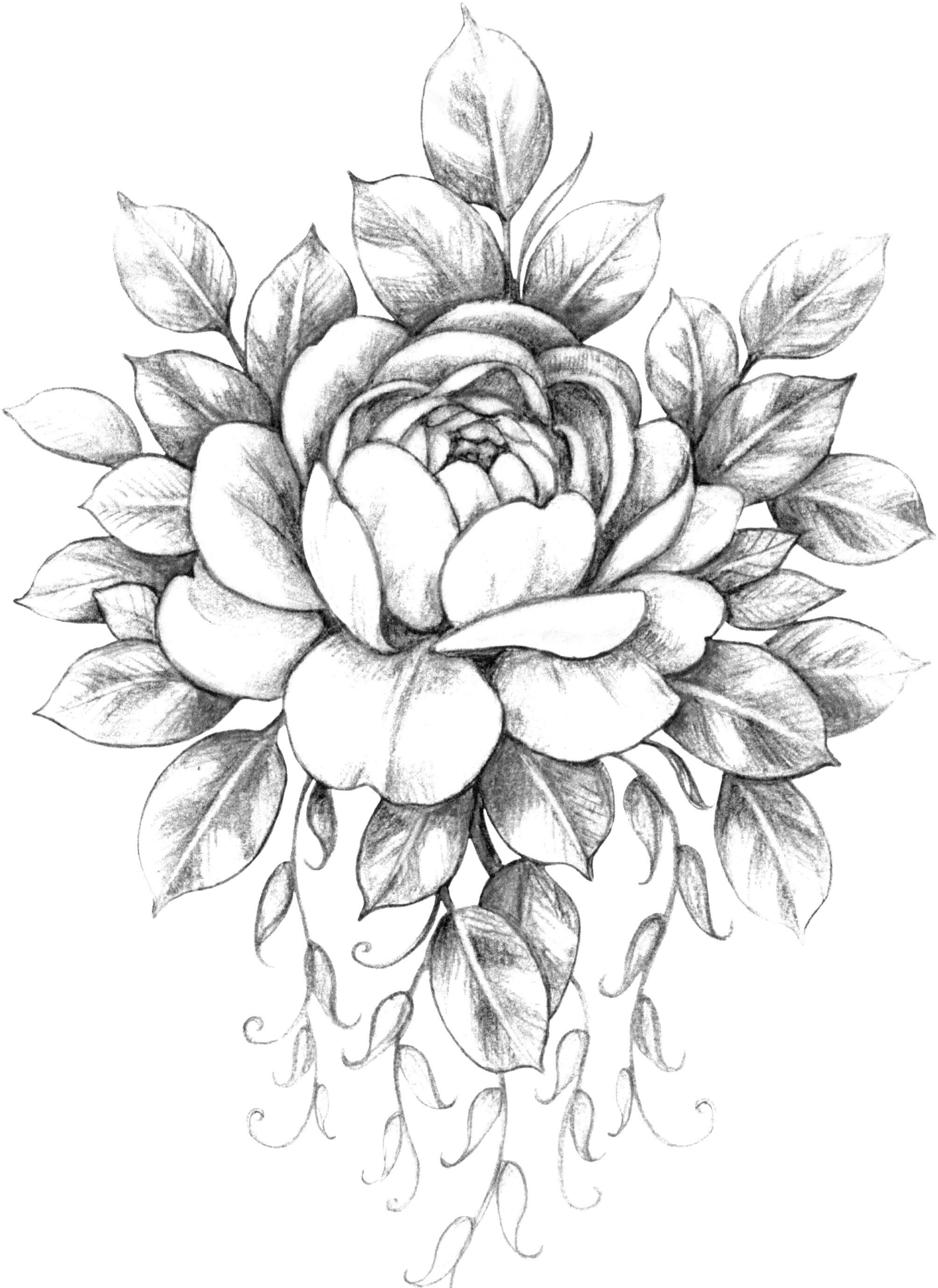

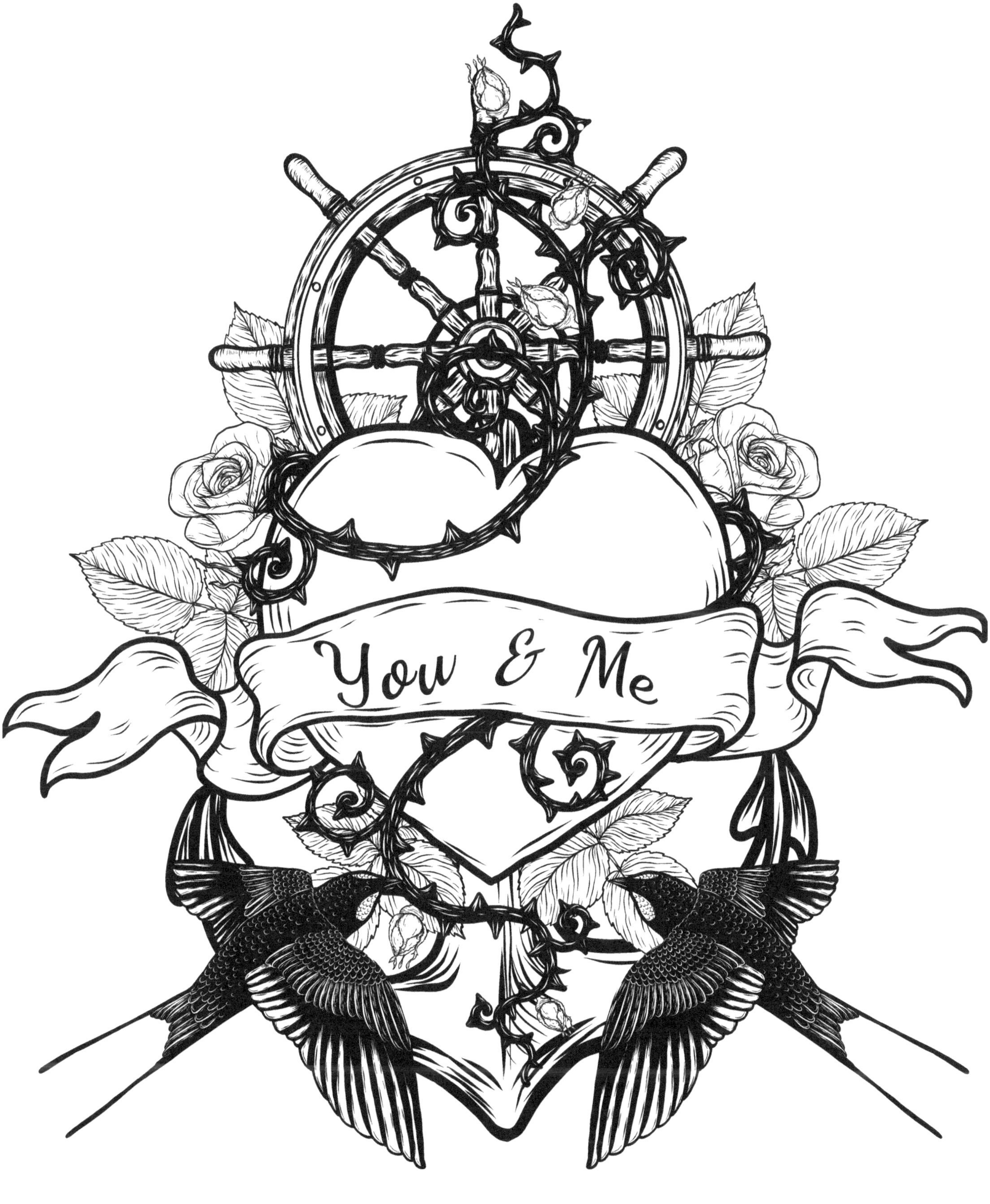
You & Me

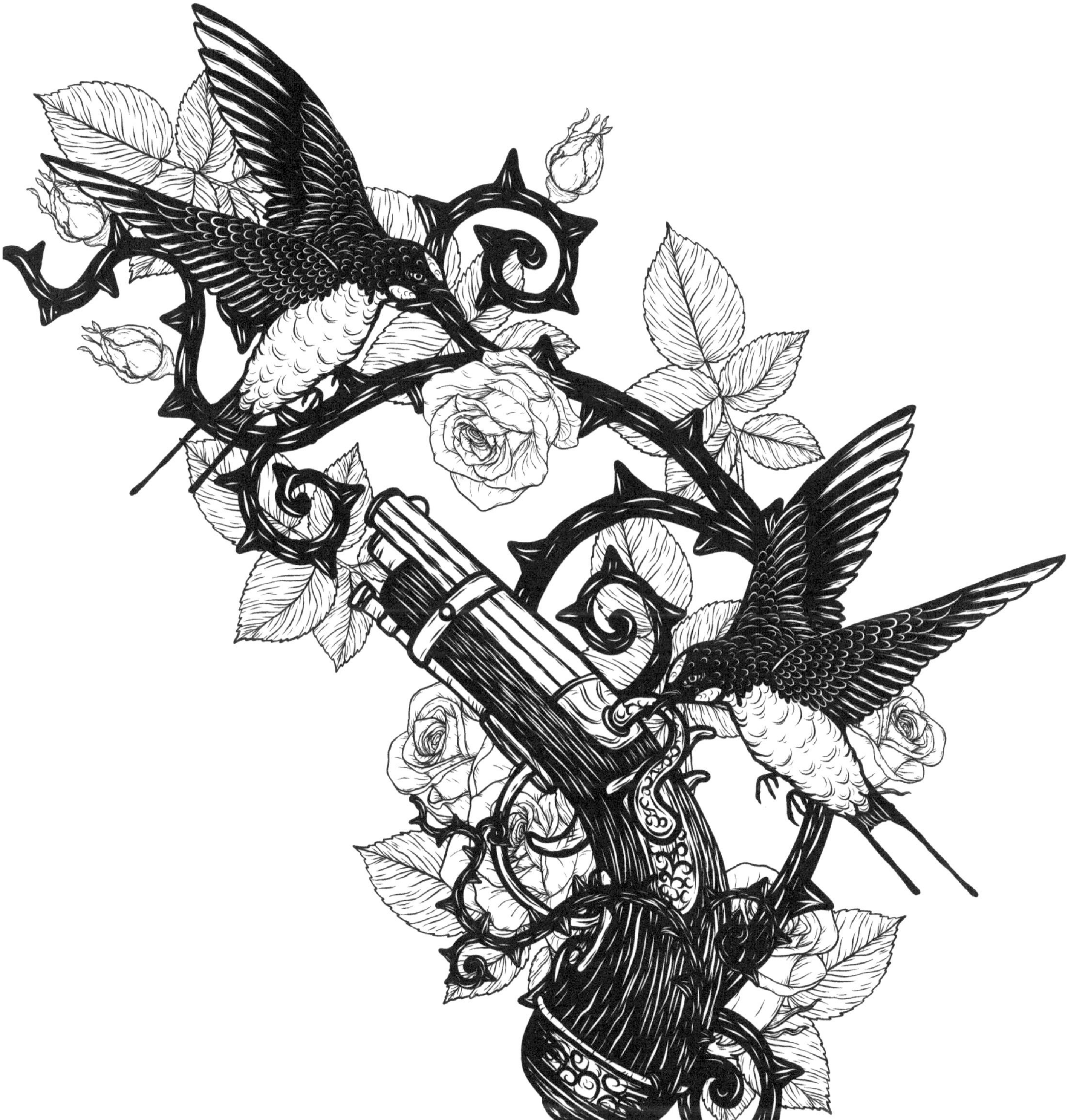

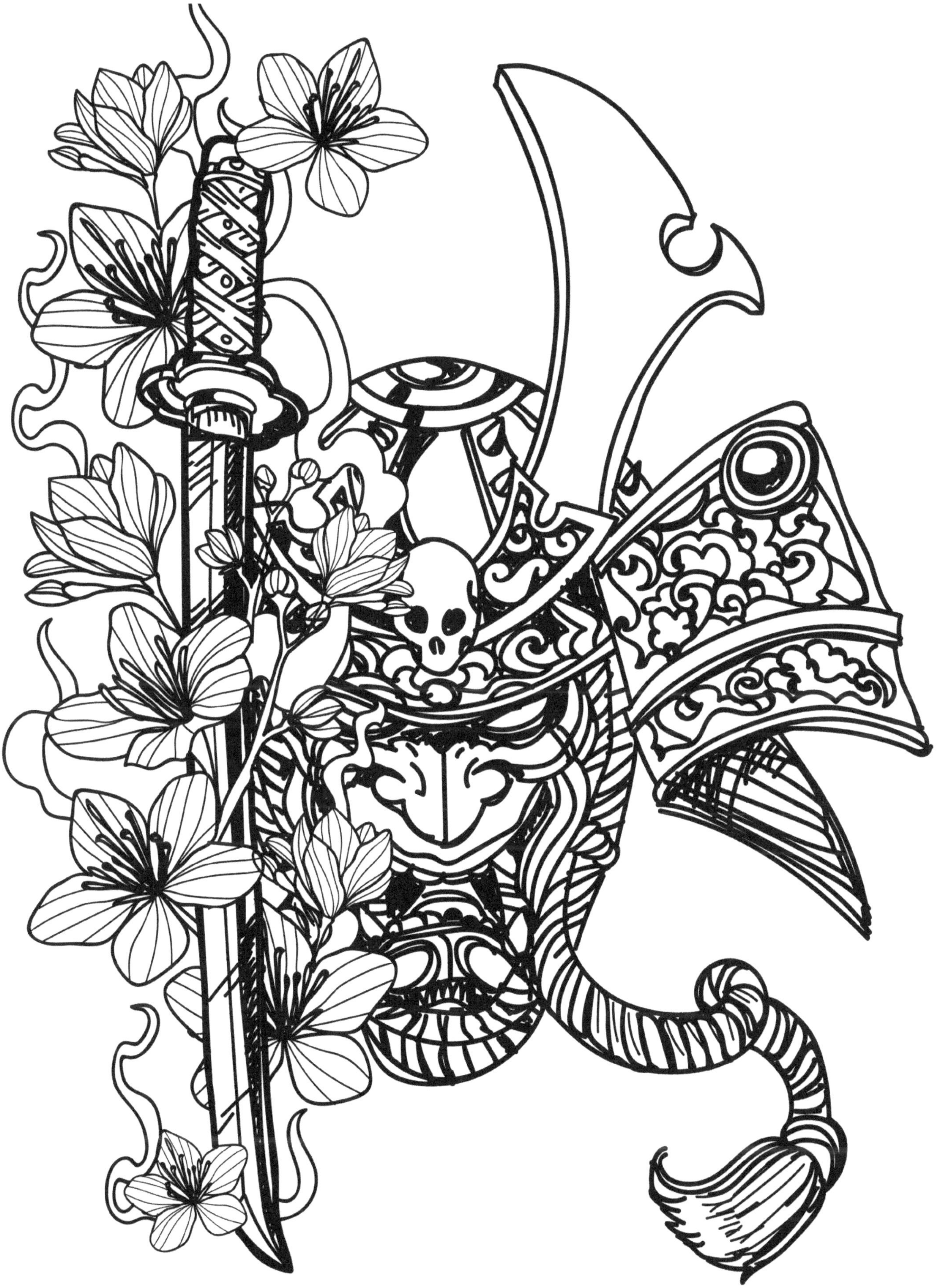

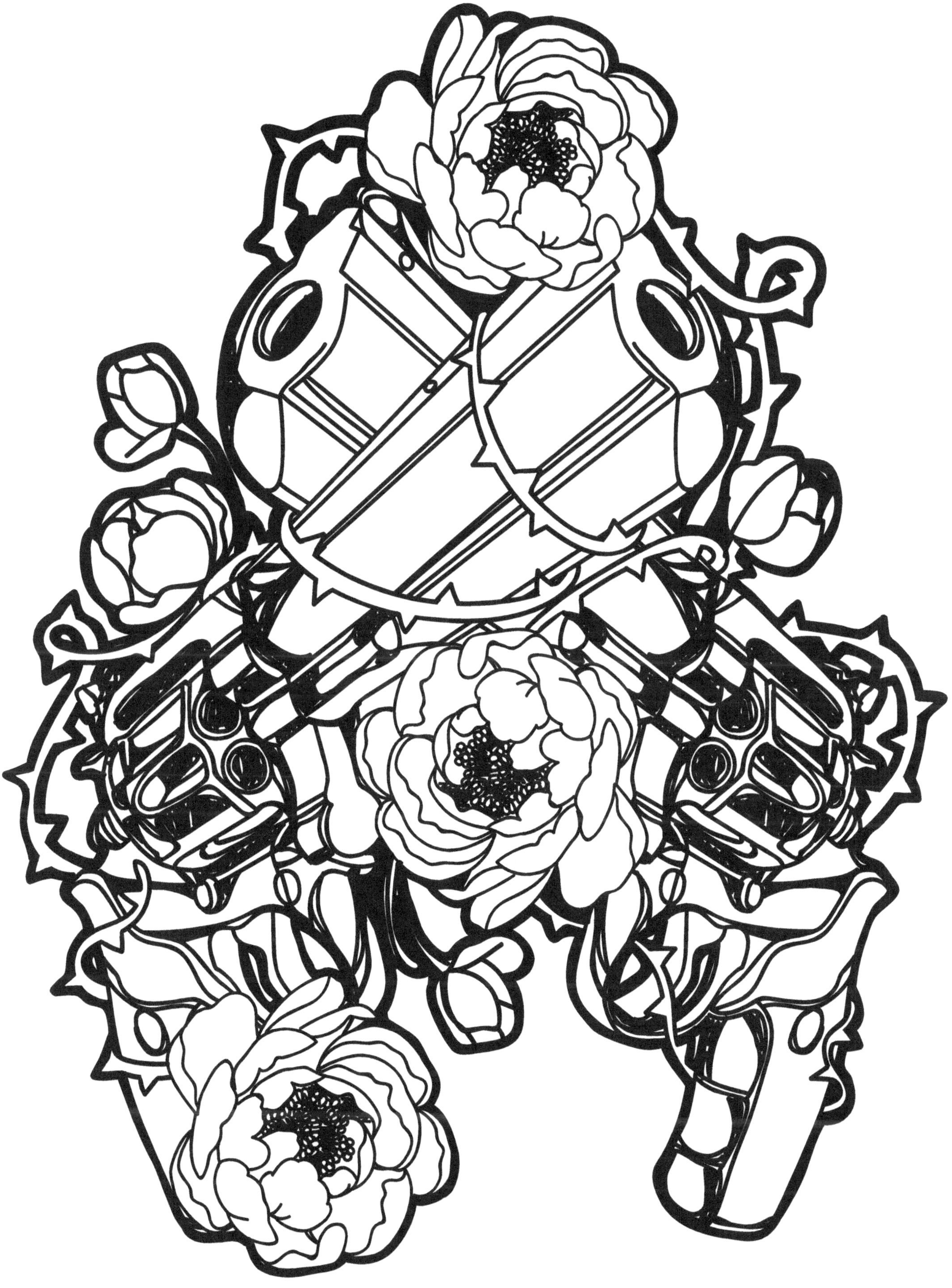

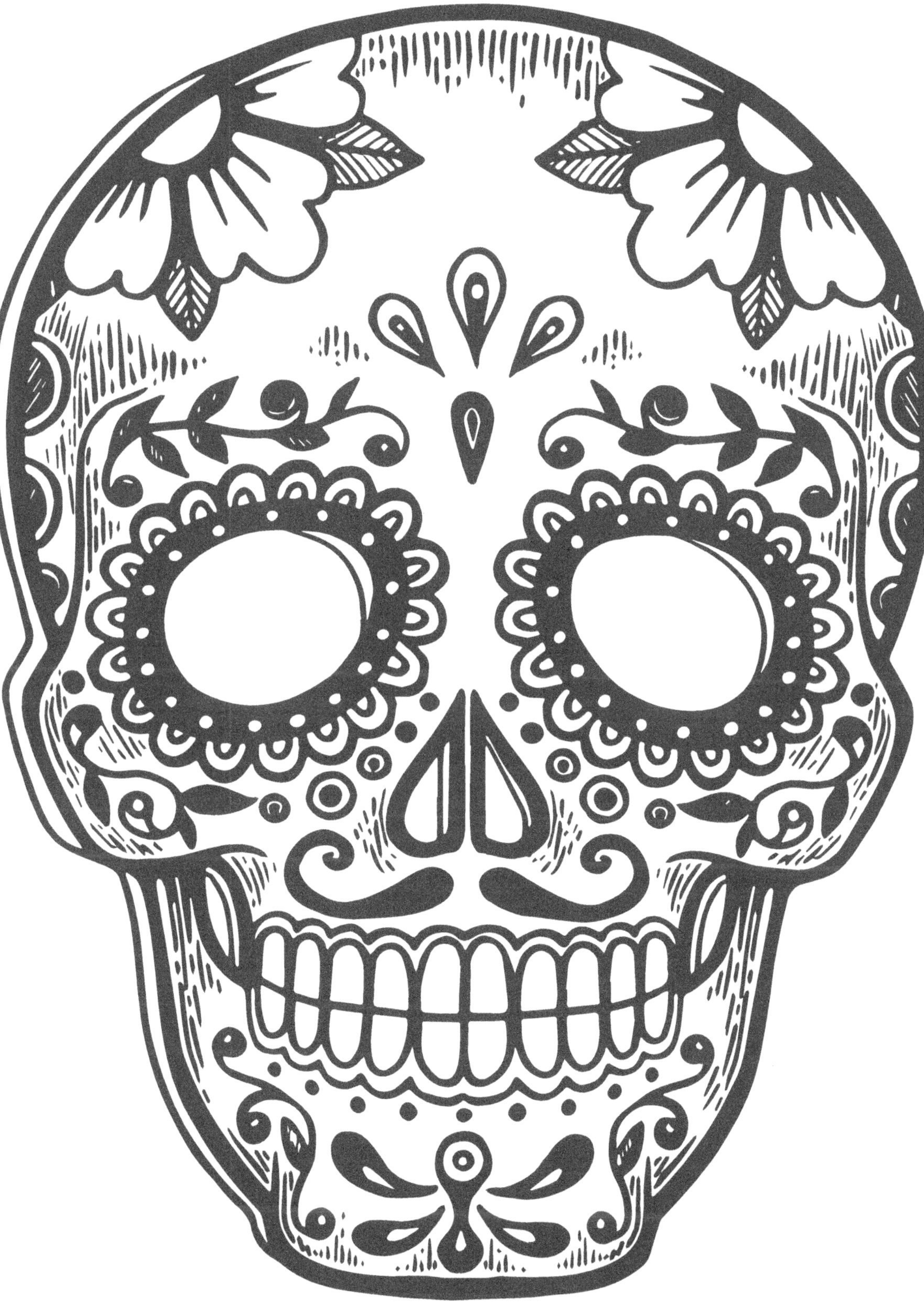

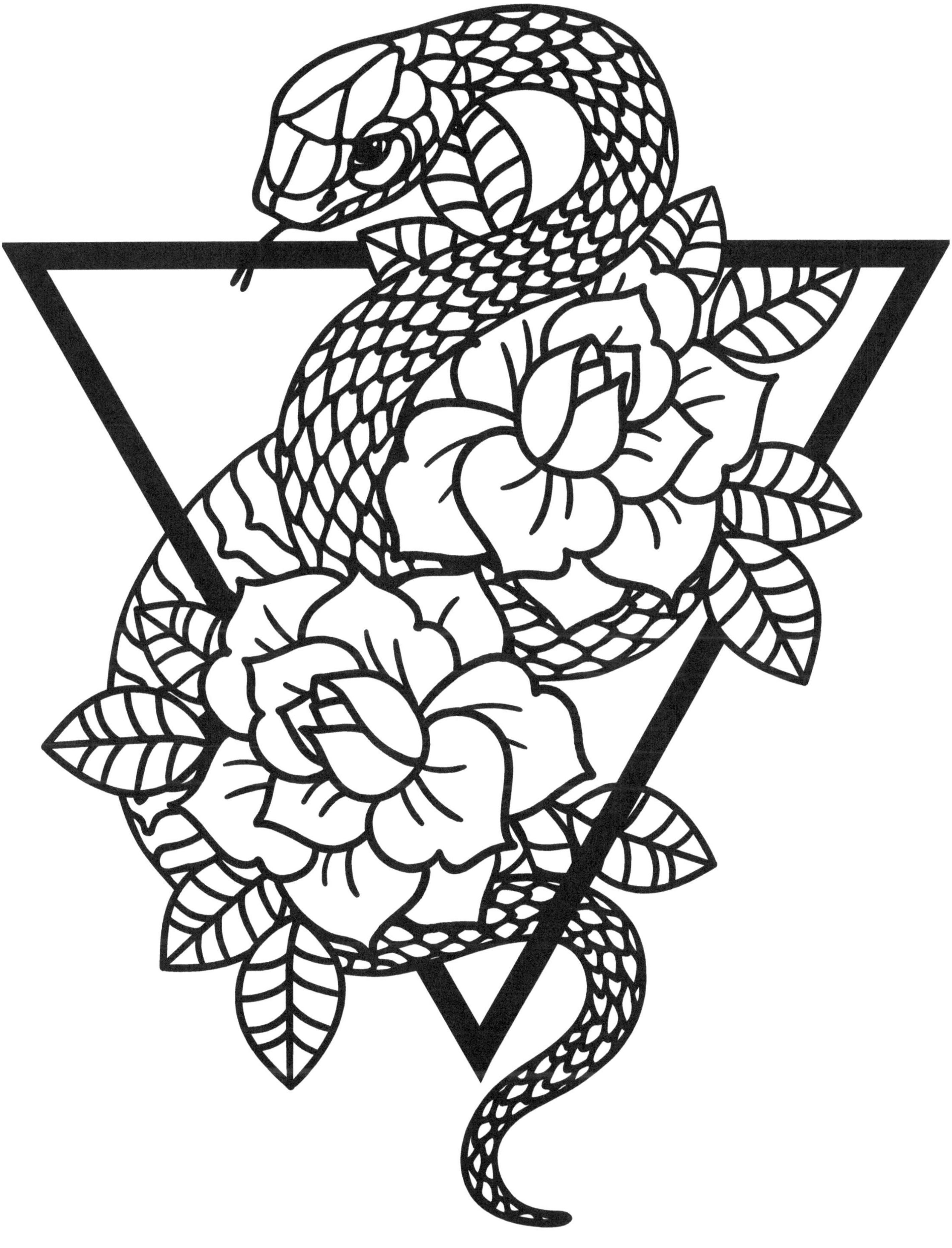

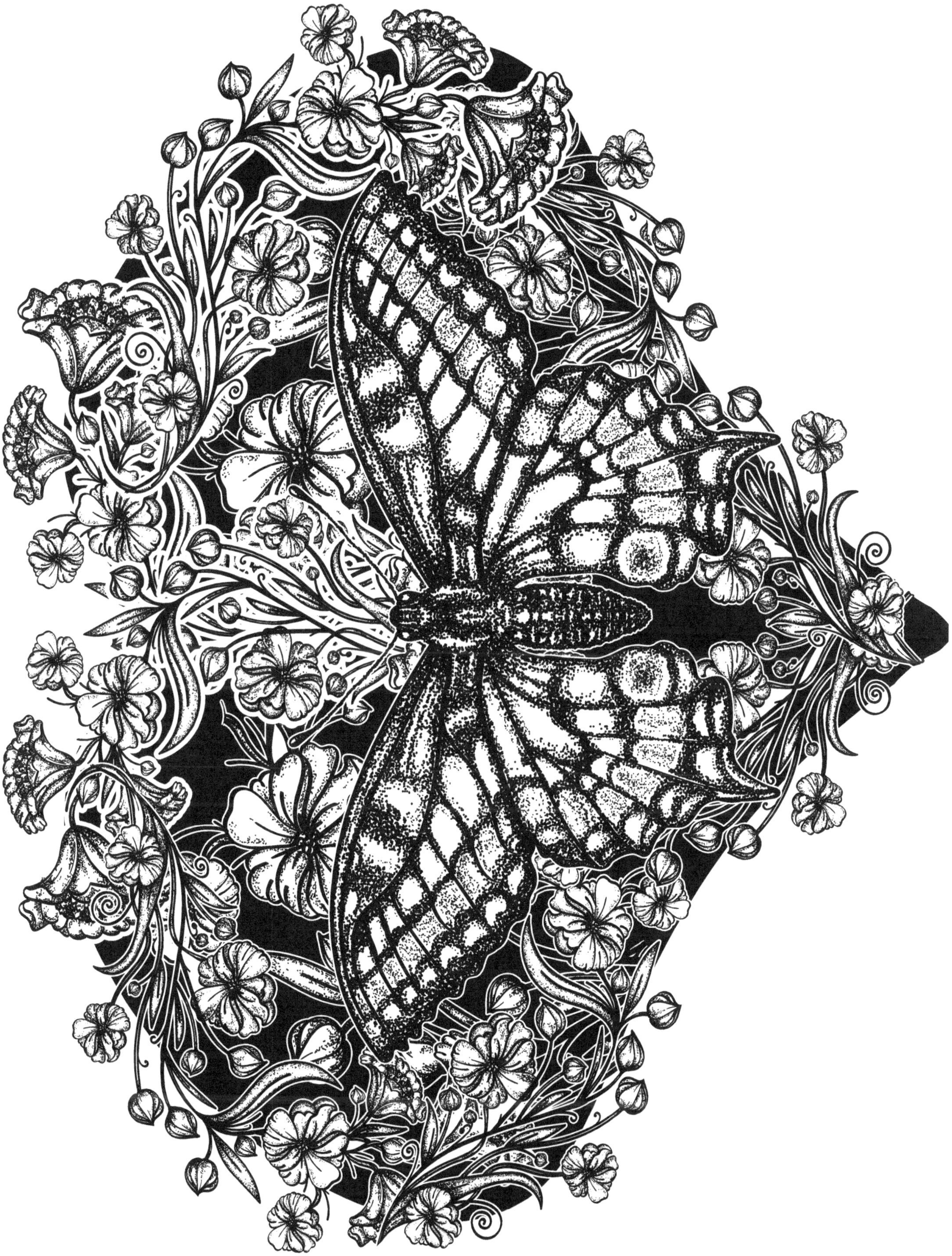

www.ingramcontent.com/pod-product-compliance
Lightning Source LLC
Chambersburg PA
CBHW081005170526
45158CB00010B/2912
* 9 7 8 1 0 8 2 4 4 3 2 7 5 *